I0427506

How to Eat Ckd Linda Blaylock

Gabriel John

Published by CEC Publisher, 2024.

HOW TO EAT CKD LINDA BLAYLOCK

First edition. March 7, 2024.

Written by Gabriel John.

Table of Contents

Introduction 1

Chapter 1 7

Chapter 2 13

Chapter 3 23

Chapter 4 33

Chapter 5 41

Chapter 6 49

Chapter 7 63

Chapter 8 71

Chapter 9 79

Chapter 10 87

Chapter 11 95

Chapter 12 103

Chapter 13 109

Conclusion 115

How to Eat Ckd Linda Blaylock

The Simple Guide to Learning Proper Ways to Eat Ckd Linda Blaylock

Gabriel John

Disclaimer

While every precaution has been taken in the preparation of this book, the publisher assumes no responsibility for errors or omissions, or for damages resulting from the use of the information contained herein.

How to Eat Ckd Linda Blaylock: The Simple Guide to Learning Proper Ways to Eat Ckd Linda Blaylock

First edition.

Table of Contents

Disclaimer

Copyright © Gabriel John 2024. All Rights Reserved

Table of Contents
Foreword
Introduction

Understanding Chronic Kidney Disease (CKD)
Importance of Nutrition in CKD Management

Chapter 1

CKD Basics
Stages of Chronic Kidney Disease
Identifying CKD Symptoms

Chapter 2

Tailoring Your Diet for CKD
Nutritional Guidelines for CKD Patients
Impact of Different Food Groups on Kidney Health

Chapter 3

Decoding Nutritional Labels
Key Elements to Look for in Labels
Making Informed Choices at the Grocery Store

Chapter 4

Meal Planning for CKD

Balancing Nutrients for Optimal Kidney Support

Sample Meal Plans for Various CKD Stages

In conclusion, "Nourishing the Kidneys" aims to empower individuals on their journey to kidney health by offering practical and delicious sample meal plans tailored to different stages of CKD. Each chapter unfolds a palette of flavors, providing not just nourishment but also enjoyment on the path to optimal kidney support. May this guide serve as a source of inspiration and culinary delight, making every meal a step toward enhanced well-being.

Chapter 5

Cooking Techniques for Kidney-Friendly Meals

Low Sodium and Low Phosphorus Cooking Tips

In conclusion, "Culinary Mastery" is more than a guide; it's a culinary adventure that invites individuals to explore the art of low sodium and low phosphorus cooking. With practical tips, delicious recipes, and thoughtful strategies, this guide empowers readers to take charge of their health while savoring the joy of flavorful meals. May this journey into the world of culinary mastery inspire and elevate the dining experience, proving that health-conscious choices can indeed be a delectable delight.

Maximizing Flavor without Compromising Health

In conclusion, "Mastering the Art" is an invitation to embark on a culinary symphony where flavor and health intertwine seamlessly. Through understanding the nuances of herbs, spices, balancing tastes, and embracing healthy fats, this guide empowers individuals to savor the richness of each bite without compromising nutritional well-being. May your culinary journey be an exploration of taste, a celebration of health, and a testament to the exquisite balance between flavor and vitality.

Chapter 6

Kidney-Approved Recipes

Breakfast

Lunch

Dinner

In conclusion, "The Culmination of Daily Nourishment" seeks to elevate dinner from a routine to a culinary symphony—a harmonious blend of flavors, nutrients, and well-being. Whether exploring global tastes, catering to dietary needs, or embracing mindful practices, this guide aims to transform dinner into a daily celebration of life's diverse and delicious possibilities. May your evenings be filled with nourishment, joy, and the satisfaction of a day well-lived.

Snacks and Desserts

In conclusion, "Indulgence with Purpose" invites readers to explore the world of snacks and desserts with a newfound appreciation for both flavor and well-being. Whether crafting nutrient-rich snacks for daily nourishment or savoring healthful desserts with intention, may this guide elevate your culinary experiences, allowing you to indulge with purpose and relish the sweetness of life.

Chapter

Hydration Strategies for CKD

Importance of Adequate Fluid Intake

In the closing pages of "Hydration Harmony," let's toast to the incredible symphony that unfolds when our bodies are in harmony with the elixir of life—water. May this exploration empower you to embrace hydration as a cornerstone of vitality, unlocking the doors to optimal well-being one sip at a time.

Choosing the Right Beverages

As we conclude our exploration into the world of beverages, I invite you to embrace the art of mindful consumption. May you navigate the diverse array of drink options with confidence, creating a harmonious symphony that not only delights your palate but also supports your journey towards a healthier and more vibrant life. Cheers to choosing beverages that truly nourish and uplift!

Chapter 8

Dining Out with CKD

Navigating Restaurant Menus

As we conclude our exploration of navigating restaurant menus, I hope this guide becomes your culinary compass, empowering you to savor each dining experience to the fullest. May your choices be both delectable and deliberate, creating memorable moments in every bite. Bon appétit!

Communicating Dietary Needs to Servers

Chapter 9

Integrating Exercise into CKD Lifestyle
Benefits of Physical Activity for Kidney Health
Safe Exercise Practices for CKD Patients

Chapter 10

Mindful Eating for Kidney Wellness

Developing Healthy Eating Habits

As we conclude this exploration of developing healthy eating habits, it is our sincere hope that this guide serves as a beacon of knowledge and inspiration. The journey to cultivating a nourishing relationship with food is a personal and transformative one. May the insights, strategies, and practical tips shared empower you on your path to nutritional mastery, fostering a lifetime of wellness and vitality. Remember, every bite is an opportunity to invest in your health and savor the joys of a vibrant and fulfilling life.

The Emotional Connection to Nutrition

Chapter 11

Monitoring and Managing CKD Progress
Regular Checkups and Lab Tests
Adjusting Your Diet According to CKD Changes

Chapter 12

Frequently Asked Questions
Common Concerns and Solutions
Expert Insights on CKD Nutrition

Chapter 13

Resources and Further Reading

Additional References for In-Depth Knowledge

Support Organizations for CKD Patients

Support organizations for CKD patients are beacons of hope, guidance, and understanding in the journey of kidney health. By offering a spectrum of services encompassing education, emotional well-being, community building, and information dissemination, these organizations contribute significantly to enhancing the lives of individuals affected by CKD. As we navigate the landscape of CKD support, these organizations serve as pillars of strength, empowering patients to face the challenges of kidney disease with resilience and knowledge.

Conclusion

Foreword

In "How to Eat CKD," Linda Blaylock has crafted an insightful and invaluable guide that transcends the boundaries of traditional dietary literature. As a seasoned expert in the field of Chronic Kidney Disease (CKD), Blaylock combines her wealth of knowledge with a compassionate understanding of the challenges individuals face when navigating a CKD-friendly diet.

This comprehensive manual not only demystifies the complexities of CKD nutrition but also empowers readers to make informed choices that enhance their well-being. Blaylock's commitment to clarity is evident as she distills intricate medical information into practical, actionable advice. From deciphering nutritional labels to crafting delicious yet kidney-friendly recipes, this book serves as an indispensable companion for those on the journey to managing CKD through mindful eating.

Blaylock's genuine concern for the reader's health permeates every page, creating a sense of trust and confidence in her guidance. "How to Eat CKD" is more than a mere dietary guide; it is a beacon of hope for those seeking a sustainable and enjoyable approach to managing CKD through wholesome nutrition.

In an era where health-conscious choices are paramount, Linda Blaylock's expertise shines through, making "How to Eat CKD" an essential resource for anyone grappling with the complexities of kidney health. As you embark on this enlightening culinary journey, may you find not only nourishment for your body but also a renewed sense of empowerment in your pursuit of a healthier life.

Introduction

Understanding Chronic Kidney Disease (CKD)

Understanding Chronic Kidney Disease (CKD): A Comprehensive Guide

Chronic Kidney Disease (CKD) is a prevalent and often silent condition that affects millions worldwide. This comprehensive guide aims to unravel the complexities of CKD, providing accurate and reliable information for individuals seeking a deeper understanding of this health challenge.

Chapter 1: Introduction

1.1 The Basics of Chronic Kidney Disease

- Definition and Stages

- Prevalence and Global Impact

1.2 Causes and Risk Factors

- Diabetes and Hypertension

- Genetic Predisposition

Chapter 2: Recognizing CKD Symptoms

2.1 Early Signs and Indicators

- Fatigue and Weakness

- Changes in Urination Patterns

2.2 Advanced Symptoms

- Swelling and Fluid Retention

- Shortness of Breath

Chapter 3: Diagnostic Processes

3.1 Screening and Early Detection

- Blood Tests and Urinalysis

- Imaging Techniques

3.2 Confirmatory Tests

- Glomerular Filtration Rate (GFR)

- Kidney Biopsy

Chapter 4: CKD Management Strategies

4.1 Lifestyle Modifications

- Dietary Changes

- Exercise and Physical Activity

4.2 Medications and Therapies

- Blood Pressure Control

- Anemia Management

Chapter 5: Dietary Guidelines for CKD Patients

5.1 Sodium and Fluid Restrictions

- Impact on Kidney Function

- Practical Tips for Reducing Intake

5.2 Protein, Phosphorus, and Potassium Balance

- Choosing Kidney-Friendly Foods

- Meal Planning for Optimal Nutrition

Chapter 6: Coping with Emotional Aspects

6.1 Psychological Impact of CKD

- Coping with Diagnosis

- Building a Support System

6.2 Maintaining Mental Health

- Stress Management

- Seeking Professional Help

Chapter 7: Looking Ahead: CKD Research and Innovations

7.1 Breakthroughs in CKD Treatment

- Advancements in Medications

- Potential Therapies on the Horizon

7.2 The Role of Technology

- Telemedicine in CKD Management

- Wearable Devices and Remote Monitoring

Conclusion: Empowering Individuals with Knowledge

In conclusion, "Understanding Chronic Kidney Disease (CKD)" strives to empower readers with accurate and accessible information. By demystifying CKD and providing practical strategies for management, this guide serves as a valuable companion for those navigating the complexities of kidney health. Knowledge is the key to proactive and informed decision-making, and this book is a vital resource for individuals on the path to better understanding and managing Chronic Kidney Disease.

Importance of Nutrition in CKD Management

THE CRUCIAL ROLE OF Nutrition in Chronic Kidney Disease (CKD) Management: A Comprehensive Guide

Nutrition plays a pivotal role in the management and well-being of individuals with Chronic Kidney Disease (CKD). This comprehensive exploration delves into the intricacies of how dietary choices can significantly impact the progression of CKD, offering insights and practical advice for those navigating this challenging journey.

CHAPTER 1: UNDERSTANDING the Foundations of Nutrition in CKD

    1.1 The Impact of Nutrition on Kidney Health

- Overview of the Renal System

- How Nutrients Interact with Kidneys

    1.2 The Link Between Diet and CKD Progression

- Role of Nutrition in Slowing Disease Advancement

- Recognizing the Early Signs of Nutritional Imbalance

CHAPTER 2: THE DYNAMICS of a Kidney-Friendly Diet

    2.1 Balancing Macronutrients for Optimal Health

- Protein Moderation in CKD

- Healthy Fats and Their Influence

    2.2 Micronutrients and CKD

- Managing Phosphorus and Potassium Intake

- The Role of Vitamins and Minerals in Renal Health

CHAPTER 3: DIETARY Strategies for CKD Stages

    3.1 Tailoring Nutrition to Different Stages of CKD

- Early Stages: Focus on Prevention
- Advanced Stages: Managing Nutritional Challenges
3.2 Personalizing Diets for Individual Needs
- Considering Coexisting Conditions
- Addressing Specific Nutritional Requirements

CHAPTER 4: FLUID MANAGEMENT for Kidney Health
4.1 The Importance of Hydration in CKD
- Balancing Fluid Intake
- Impact of Dehydration on Kidney Function
4.2 Choosing the Right Beverages
- Tea, Coffee, and Their Effects
- The Role of Water in Hydration

CHAPTER 5: PRACTICAL Tips for Incorporating Kidney-Friendly Foods
5.1 Grocery Shopping for CKD Patients
- Reading Nutrition Labels Effectively
- Identifying Hidden Sodium and Phosphorus
5.2 Cooking Techniques for Nutrient Retention
- Kidney-Friendly Cooking Methods
- Enhancing Flavor Without Compromising Health

CHAPTER 6: CHALLENGES and Solutions in CKD Nutrition
6.1 Overcoming Dietary Restrictions
- Strategies for Coping with Limited Food Choices
- Incorporating Variety in a Restricted Diet
6.2 Social and Emotional Aspects of Dietary Changes
- Navigating Social Gatherings and Restaurants

- Psychological Impact of Altered Eating Habits

CHAPTER 7: THE EVOLVING Landscape of Nutritional Research in CKD
7.1 Current Research Trends
- Breakthroughs in Nutritional Approaches
- Promising Dietary Interventions on the Horizon
7.2 The Intersection of Technology and Nutrition
- Apps and Tools for Tracking Nutrient Intake
- Wearable Devices in Monitoring Dietary Impact

CONCLUSION: EMPOWERING Through Informed Nutrition

In conclusion, recognizing the importance of nutrition in CKD management is a critical step towards enhancing the quality of life for individuals facing this health challenge. This comprehensive guide aims to provide accurate information, dispel myths, and empower readers with practical strategies for adopting a kidney-friendly lifestyle. By understanding the profound impact of nutrition on CKD, individuals can take proactive steps to optimize their dietary choices and positively influence their renal health journey.

Chapter 1

CKD Basics

Stages of Chronic Kidney Disease

Navigating the Landscape of Chronic Kidney Disease (CKD): A Detailed Exploration of its Stages

Chronic Kidney Disease (CKD) is a complex and progressive condition that demands a nuanced understanding of its various stages. This comprehensive exploration aims to provide accurate insights into the stages of CKD, offering detailed information that is essential for individuals, caregivers, and healthcare professionals alike.

CHAPTER 1: INTRODUCTION to Chronic Kidney Disease

    1.1 Defining Chronic Kidney Disease

    - Understanding Kidney Function

    - The Pervasiveness of CKD Worldwide

    1.2 The Silent Progression of CKD

    - Early Detection Challenges

    - The Importance of Timely Diagnosis

CHAPTER 2: STAGE 1: Early Kidney Damage

    2.1 Recognizing the First Signs

    - Importance of Regular Checkups

    - Identifying Elevated Kidney Markers

    2.2 Strategies for Halting Progression

    - Lifestyle Modifications in Stage 1

- Monitoring Blood Pressure and Blood Sugar Levels

CHAPTER 3: STAGE 2: Mild Decline in Kidney Function
  3.1 Progression and Risk Factors
  - Factors Contributing to Stage 2
  - Addressing Underlying Causes
  3.2 Diet and Lifestyle Adjustments
  - Role of Nutrition in Slowing Progression
  - Exercise and Physical Activity Recommendations

CHAPTER 4: STAGE 3: Moderate Decline and the Importance of Management
  4.1 Navigating the Challenges of Moderate Kidney Decline
  - Recognizing Symptoms in Stage 3
  - Emphasizing Medication Adherence
  4.2 Renal Nutrition in Stage 3
  - Dietary Adjustments for Optimal Kidney Support
  - Collaborative Care Between Patients and Healthcare Providers

CHAPTER 5: STAGE 4: Severe Decline and Preparation for Advanced CKD
  5.1 Addressing the Growing Impact on Daily Life
  - Managing Symptoms in Stage 4
  - Psychological Support for Patients and Caregivers
  5.2 Considerations for Future Treatments
  - Exploring Dialysis Options
  - Evaluating Transplant Eligibility

CHAPTER 6: STAGE 5: End-Stage Kidney Disease (ESKD) and Treatment Options

6.1 Understanding the Transition to ESKD

- Identifying Symptoms of ESKD

- The Role of Dialysis in Advanced CKD

6.2 Transplantation as a Viable Solution

- The Transplant Evaluation Process

- Post-Transplant Care and Lifestyle Adjustments

CONCLUSION: EMPOWERING Individuals Through Knowledge

In conclusion, the stages of Chronic Kidney Disease form a spectrum that necessitates tailored approaches at each phase. This comprehensive guide strives to illuminate the nuances of each stage, providing invaluable insights for individuals, caregivers, and healthcare professionals alike. By understanding the progression of CKD and embracing proactive measures, we can collectively contribute to enhancing the quality of life for those navigating this intricate journey.

Identifying CKD Symptoms

UNMASKING THE SIGNS: A Comprehensive Guide to Identifying Chronic Kidney Disease Symptoms

Understanding the early indicators of Chronic Kidney Disease (CKD) is crucial for timely diagnosis and effective management. This in-depth exploration sheds light on the subtle yet significant symptoms that may signal the presence of CKD, empowering individuals to take proactive steps towards kidney health.

CHAPTER 1: THE SILENT Progression of CKD
    1.1 Unveiling the Stealthy Nature of CKD
    - Why CKD Often Goes Unnoticed
    - The Importance of Regular Health Checkups
    1.2 The Significance of Early Detection
    - Impact on Treatment Outcomes
    - Reducing the Burden of Advanced Kidney Disease

CHAPTER 2: GENERAL Indicators of Kidney Dysfunction
    2.1 Changes in Urination Patterns
    - Frequency and Color Changes
    - Recognizing Unexplained Urgency
    2.2 Fluid Retention and Swelling
    - Understanding Edema
    - Noticing Changes in Facial Appearance and Extremities

CHAPTER 3: FATIGUE and Weakness: Unraveling Their Kidney Connection

3.1 Debilitating Impact on Daily Life
- The Nuances of CKD-Related Fatigue
- Addressing Weakness and Lethargy
3.2 Differentiating CKD Fatigue from Routine Tiredness
- Persistent vs. Occasional Fatigue
- When to Seek Medical Attention

CHAPTER 4: ANEMIA AND Its Relationship to Kidney Function
4.1 Understanding Anemia in CKD
- Impact on Oxygen Transport
- Identifying Pale Skin and Fatigue as Anemia Indicators
4.2 The Role of Erythropoietin (EPO) Deficiency
- How CKD Affects EPO Production
- Treatment Options for CKD-Related Anemia

CHAPTER 5: HIGH BLOOD Pressure as a Silent Culprit
5.1 The Interplay Between CKD and Hypertension
- How Hypertension Contributes to Kidney Damage
- Monitoring Blood Pressure as a Preventive Measure
5.2 Unmasking Silent Hypertension Symptoms
- Headaches and Dizziness
- Vision Changes and Nosebleeds

CHAPTER 6: EVALUATING Bone Health and CKD
6.1 The Impact of Phosphorus Imbalance
- Bone Pain and Weakness
- Dental Issues as Warning Signs
6.2 Recognizing CKD-Mineral and Bone Disorder (CKD-MBD)

- Radiographic Changes in Bones
- Managing Phosphorus Levels for Optimal Bone Health

CHAPTER 7: THE EMOTIONAL Toll of CKD
7.1 Understanding the Psychological Impact
- Anxiety and Depression in CKD Patients
- Strategies for Coping with Emotional Distress
7.2 Seeking Professional Support
- Importance of Mental Health in CKD Management
- Collaborative Care Between Healthcare Providers and Mental Health Professionals

CONCLUSION: A CALL to Action for Kidney Health

In conclusion, recognizing the symptoms of Chronic Kidney Disease is the first step towards proactive and effective management. This comprehensive guide seeks to empower individuals with the knowledge needed to identify subtle signs, enabling early intervention and improved outcomes. By understanding the nuances of CKD symptoms, we pave the way for a healthier and more informed approach to kidney health.

Chapter 2

Tailoring Your Diet for CKD

Nutritional Guidelines for CKD Patients

Navigating the Plate: Nutritional Guidelines for Optimal Chronic Kidney Disease (CKD) Management

Understanding and adhering to proper nutritional guidelines is paramount for individuals managing Chronic Kidney Disease (CKD). This comprehensive guide provides accurate insights and practical advice, empowering patients to make informed dietary choices for kidney health.

CHAPTER 1: THE FOUNDATIONS of a Kidney-Friendly Diet
    1.1 Unveiling the Importance of Nutrition in CKD
    - How Diet Impacts Kidney Function
    - The Role of Nutrition in Slowing CKD Progression
    1.2 Building a Balanced Plate for Kidney Health
    - Macronutrient Moderation: Protein, Fats, and Carbohydrates
    - Micronutrient Focus: Vitamins and Minerals

CHAPTER 2: PROTEIN Moderation: A Key Aspect in CKD Nutrition
    2.1 Understanding the Impact of Protein on Kidney Function
    - Balancing Protein Intake in Different CKD Stages
    - Sources of High-Quality Proteins for CKD Patients
    2.2 Navigating Protein-Restricted Diets
    - Dietary Approaches to Manage Protein Intake
    - Addressing Protein-Energy Wasting in Advanced CKD

CHAPTER 3: MANAGING Phosphorus and Potassium Levels

    3.1 The Critical Role of Phosphorus in CKD Nutrition

    - Phosphorus-Rich Foods to Limit

    - Phosphate Binders: A Tool in Phosphorus Control

    3.2 Potassium Balance in CKD

    - Monitoring Potassium Intake

    - Low-Potassium Food Choices for CKD Patients

CHAPTER 4: SODIUM AND Fluid Restrictions for Kidney Health

    4.1 Unveiling the Impact of Sodium on CKD Progression

    - The Connection Between Sodium and Blood Pressure

    - Strategies for Reducing Sodium Intake

    4.2 Navigating Fluid Intake

    - The Importance of Fluid Balance in CKD

    - Practical Tips for Managing Fluid Intake

CHAPTER 5: CRAFTING Kidney-Friendly Meals and Snacks

    5.1 Breakfast Ideas for CKD Patients

    - Nutrient-Dense Breakfast Choices

    - Creative and Flavorful Options

    5.2 Lunch, Dinner, and Snacking Strategies

    - Building Balanced Meals

    - Snack Ideas That Align with CKD Guidelines

CHAPTER 6: COOKING Techniques for Optimal Nutrient Retention

    6.1 Low Sodium and Low Phosphorus Cooking Tips

- Flavor Enhancement Without Compromising Health
- The Art of Herbs and Spices in Kidney-Friendly Cooking
6.2 Maximizing Flavor Without Compromising Health
- Culinary Techniques to Enhance Taste
- Meal Planning for Variety and Nutritional Balance

CHAPTER 7: DINING OUT with CKD
  7.1 Navigating Restaurant Menus
  - Communication with Restaurant Staff
  - Making Informed Choices When Eating Out
  7.2 Handling Social Situations and Gatherings
  - Strategies for Socializing While Adhering to CKD Guidelines
  - Celebrating Special Occasions Mindfully

CHAPTER 8: THE EVOLVING Landscape of CKD Nutrition Research
  8.1 Current Trends in CKD Dietary Research
  - Innovations in Nutritional Approaches
  - Potential Breakthroughs on the Horizon
  8.2 Integrating Technology in CKD Dietary Management
  - Apps and Tools for Nutrient Tracking
  - Wearable Devices and Remote Monitoring in Nutrition

CONCLUSION: A PATH to Optimal Kidney Health Through Informed Nutrition

In conclusion, "Navigating the Plate" serves as a comprehensive guide to empower individuals managing CKD through informed and practical nutritional choices. By understanding the nuances of a kidney-friendly diet and embracing a holistic approach to nutrition, readers can take proactive steps toward optimizing their kidney health and enhancing their overall well-being.

Impact of Different Food Groups on Kidney Health

UNVEILING THE CULINARY Canvas: The Impact of Different Food Groups on Kidney Health

In the intricate tapestry of managing kidney health, the foods we consume play a pivotal role. This comprehensive exploration delves into the nuanced impact of various food groups on kidney function, offering insights and expert guidance for individuals navigating the delicate balance between flavor and renal well-being.

CHAPTER 1: UNDERSTANDING the Interplay Between Diet and Kidney Health
1.1 The Role of Nutrition in Renal Function
- How Dietary Choices Affect Kidney Health
- Recognizing the Impact of Different Nutrients
1.2 The Complex Relationship Between Food Groups and CKD
- Carbohydrates, Proteins, Fats, and Their Varied Effects
- The Synergy of a Balanced Diet for Optimal Kidney Support

CHAPTER 2: THE PROTEIN Dilemma: Moderation and Quality
2.1 Unraveling the Protein Conundrum in Kidney Health
- The Significance of Protein in Renal Function
- Navigating Protein Moderation in Different Stages of CKD
2.2 Optimal Sources of High-Quality Proteins
- Animal vs. Plant-Based Proteins
- Creating a Protein-Optimized Diet for Kidney Health

CHAPTER 3: BALANCING Carbohydrates for Kidney-Friendly Nutrition

3.1 The Impact of Carbohydrates on Blood Sugar and Kidneys

- Understanding Glycemic Index and Kidney Health
- Carbohydrates in the Context of Diabetes and CKD

3.2 The Fiber Connection

- Dietary Fiber's Role in Kidney Function
- Choosing Complex Carbohydrates for Sustained Energy

CHAPTER 4: FATS: NAVIGATING the Heart-Healthy Choices

4.1 The Dichotomy of Fats and Kidney Health

- The Importance of Essential Fatty Acids
- Saturated vs. Unsaturated Fats in CKD

4.2 Incorporating Heart-Healthy Fats into the Renal Diet

- Omega-3 Fatty Acids and Their Renal Benefits
- Making Informed Choices for Cooking Oils

CHAPTER 5: MICRONUTRIENTS: The Vital Role of Vitamins and Minerals

5.1 The Micronutrient Landscape in Kidney Health

- Essential Vitamins for Renal Function
- Minerals and Their Impact on Electrolyte Balance

5.2 Dietary Approaches to Phosphorus and Potassium Control

- Managing Phosphorus Intake Through Food Choices
- Balancing Potassium for Optimal Kidney Support

CHAPTER 6: SODIUM SENSITIVITY: The Crucial Connection to Kidney Function

    6.1 Sodium and Its Influence on Kidney Health

    - Understanding Sodium's Role in Fluid Balance

    - The Impact of Excess Sodium on Blood Pressure

    6.2 Practical Tips for Sodium Reduction

    - Reading Food Labels Effectively

    - Flavoring Foods Without Excessive Salt

CHAPTER 7: FLUID DYNAMICS: The Importance of Hydration in Kidney Care

    7.1 Hydration and Its Crucial Role in Renal Function

    - The Link Between Dehydration and Kidney Strain

    - Fluid Intake Recommendations for Different CKD Stages

    7.2 Choosing the Right Beverages for Optimal Kidney Health

    - The Impact of Caffeine and Alcohol on Kidney Function

    - Hydration Strategies Beyond Water

CHAPTER 8: CRAFTING Kidney-Friendly Meals: Practical Tips and Recipes

    8.1 Breakfast Ideas for Kidney Health

    - Nutrient-Dense and Flavorful Morning Options

    - Balancing Proteins, Carbs, and Fats in Breakfast Meals

    8.2 Lunch, Dinner, and Snacking Strategies

    - Creating Balanced and Flavorful Meals

    - Snack Ideas Aligned with Kidney Health

CHAPTER 9: CULTURAL Considerations: Tailoring Diets for Individual Needs

    9.1 Embracing Diversity in Dietary Choices

    - Cultural Influences on Food Preferences

    - Adapting Traditional Diets for Kidney Health

    9.2 Personalizing Diets for Coexisting Conditions

    - Addressing the Intersection of CKD with Other Health Conditions

    - Collaborative Care Between Patients and Healthcare Providers

CHAPTER 10: NAVIGATING Dietary Challenges in Social and Special Occasions

    10.1 Strategies for Socializing While Adhering to CKD Guidelines

    - Navigating Restaurants and Social Gatherings

    - Celebrating Special Occasions Mindfully

    10.2 Mindful Eating: A Holistic Approach to Nutrition

    - The Emotional Connection to Food

    - Strategies for Coping with Emotional Eating

CHAPTER 11: THE EVOLVING Landscape of Nutritional Research in Kidney Health

    11.1 Current Research Trends in CKD Nutrition

    - Innovations in Nutritional Approaches

    - Potential Breakthroughs in Dietary Interventions

    11.2 The Intersection of Technology and Nutrition

    - Apps and Tools for Nutrient Tracking

    - Wearable Devices in Monitoring Dietary Impact

CONCLUSION: A CULINARY Compass for Kidney Wellness

In conclusion, "Unveiling the Culinary Canvas" seeks to empower individuals with a comprehensive understanding of the impact of different food groups on kidney health. By navigating the intricacies of protein, carbohydrates, fats, and micronutrients, readers can craft a culinary compass for optimal renal function. This guide serves as a roadmap to informed dietary choices, embracing the delicate balance between flavor and kidney wellness.

Chapter 3

Decoding Nutritional Labels

Key Elements to Look for in Labels

DECODING LABELS: A Comprehensive Guide to Key Elements for Informed Choices

In the modern landscape of grocery shopping, deciphering food labels has become a crucial skill for individuals striving to make informed and healthy choices. This in-depth exploration will unravel the intricacies of food labels, empowering consumers to navigate the aisles with confidence and make choices aligned with their nutritional goals.

CHAPTER 1: THE BASICS of Food Labels

    1.1 Understanding the Purpose of Food Labels

    - Legal Requirements and Consumer Protection

    - How Labels Contribute to Informed Decision-Making

    1.2 Navigating the Components of a Food Label

    - Breaking Down the Nutrition Facts Panel

    - Other Key Information on Packaging

CHAPTER 2: SERVING Size: The Foundation of Nutritional Information

    2.1 Significance of Serving Size in Nutritional Context

    - Defining Standard Servings

- Impact of Serving Size on Daily Nutrient Intake
2.2 Practical Application of Serving Size Information
- Adjusting Portion Sizes for Individual Needs
- Avoiding Common Pitfalls in Serving Size Interpretation

CHAPTER 3: CALORIC Content: Balancing Energy Intake
3.1 Deciphering Caloric Information on Labels
- Understanding Caloric Needs
- Interpreting Caloric Content in the Context of a Balanced Diet
3.2 Impact of Macronutrients on Caloric Content
- Caloric Distribution from Carbohydrates, Proteins, and Fats
- Making Informed Choices Based on Caloric Composition

CHAPTER 4: NUTRIENT Breakdown: Unveiling the Core Elements
4.1 Analyzing Macronutrients: Carbohydrates, Proteins, and Fats
- The Role of Carbohydrates in Energy Provision
- Protein Quality and Quantity Considerations
- Balancing Healthy Fats for Optimal Nutrition
4.2 Micronutrients: Vitamins and Minerals in Focus
- Essential Micronutrients and Their Contributions
- Evaluating Micronutrient Percentages on Labels

CHAPTER 5: DIETARY Fiber and Sugar Content: Impact on Health
5.1 The Crucial Role of Dietary Fiber in the Diet
- Types of Dietary Fiber and Their Benefits
- Evaluating Fiber Content on Labels
5.2 Navigating the Sugar Conundrum
- Differentiating Natural and Added Sugars

- Interpreting Sugar Content in the Context of Health Guidelines

CHAPTER 6: SODIUM LEVELS: Unmasking Hidden Salt
6.1 The Relationship Between Sodium and Health
- Daily Sodium Recommendations
- Identifying Hidden Sodium in Processed Foods
6.2 Making Informed Choices for Sodium Intake
- Opting for Low-Sodium Alternatives
- Reducing Overall Sodium Intake for Heart and Kidney Health

CHAPTER 7: INGREDIENT List: Decoding What Goes into Your Food
7.1 The Significance of Reading Ingredient Lists
- Identifying Key Ingredients in a Product
- Recognizing Common Additives and Preservatives
7.2 Prioritizing Whole and Natural Ingredients
- The Benefits of a Clean and Minimally Processed Ingredient List
- Red Flags: Ingredients to Approach with Caution

CHAPTER 8: ALLERGEN Information: Ensuring Safety
8.1 The Importance of Allergen Labeling
- Common Allergens and Their Prevalence
- Interpreting Allergen Warnings on Labels
8.2 Strategies for Allergen-Free Shopping
- Reading Labels Thoroughly to Avoid Allergens
- Navigating Cross-Contamination Risks

CHAPTER 9: CERTIFICATION Labels: Trusting Verified Standards

9.1 Recognizing Certifications and Seals on Packaging

- Understanding Labels Such as USDA Organic, Non-GMO, and Gluten-Free

- The Rigorous Standards Behind Certification Labels

9.2 Making Ethical and Sustainable Choices

- Impact of Certifications on Environmental and Social Responsibility

- Balancing Health and Sustainability in Consumer Choices

CHAPTER 10: INTERPRETING Marketing Claims: Differentiating Fact from Fiction

10.1 The World of Marketing Buzzwords

- "Natural," "Healthy," and Other Common Claims

- Scrutinizing Marketing Language for Informed Choices

10.2 Understanding Regulatory Limits and Oversight

- Limits on Marketing Claims and Misleading Statements

- Reporting Suspected Misrepresentation to Regulatory Agencies

CHAPTER 11: SMART SHOPPING Strategies: Putting Knowledge into Practice

11.1 Creating a Practical Shopping Checklist

- Preparing Before You Shop

- Efficiently Navigating the Grocery Store

11.2 Tips for Comparing and Selecting Products

- Identifying Healthier Alternatives

- Making Budget-Friendly and Nutrient-Dense Choices

CONCLUSION: EMPOWERING Consumers Through Label Literacy

In conclusion, "Decoding Labels" serves as an essential guide for consumers seeking to navigate the labyrinth of food labels with confidence and clarity. By understanding the key elements on labels, individuals can make informed choices aligned with their nutritional goals, fostering a healthier and more mindful approach to food consumption. This comprehensive exploration empowers consumers to take control of their dietary decisions and advocate for their well-being in an increasingly complex and diverse marketplace.

Making Informed Choices at the Grocery Store

NAVIGATING THE AISLES: A Guide to Making Informed Choices at the Grocery Store

Embarking on a journey to make healthier and informed choices at the grocery store is a significant step towards a balanced and nourishing lifestyle. This comprehensive guide is designed to empower individuals with the knowledge and strategies needed to navigate the aisles with confidence, ensuring that every trip to the grocery store becomes an opportunity for optimal well-being.

CHAPTER 1: THE FOUNDATION of Informed Shopping
    1.1 The Importance of Preparation Before You Shop
    - Creating a Shopping List Based on Nutritional Goals
    - Understanding Dietary Requirements for Individual Health
    1.2 Practical Tips for Smart and Efficient Grocery Shopping
    - Organizing Your Shopping List by Aisle
    - Timing Your Shopping Trip for Convenience and Freshness

CHAPTER 2: READING and Understanding Food Labels
    2.1 Deciphering Nutrition Facts Panels
    - Interpreting Serving Sizes and Calories
    - Understanding Percent Daily Values

2.2 Analyzing Ingredient Lists and Recognizing Red Flags
- Identifying Hidden Sugars and Artificial Additives
- Prioritizing Whole and Natural Ingredients

CHAPTER 3: STRATEGIC Placement of Essential Foods in Your Cart
3.1 Prioritizing Fresh Produce and Seasonal Options
- The Benefits of a Colorful and Diverse Produce Selection
- Choosing Locally Sourced and Seasonal Fruits and Vegetables
3.2 Navigating the Protein Aisle for Optimal Choices
- Selecting Lean Protein Sources
- Exploring Plant-Based Protein Alternatives

CHAPTER 4: WHOLE GRAINS and Carbohydrates: Balancing Nutrient
Density
4.1 The Role of Whole Grains in a Balanced Diet
- Identifying Whole Grain Products
- Understanding the Impact of Carbohydrates on Blood Sugar
4.2 Choosing Smart Carbohydrates for Energy and Satiety
- Opting for Fiber-Rich and Low-Glycemic Options
- Integrating Variety in Grain Choices

CHAPTER 5: FATS AND Oils: Selecting Heart-Healthy Options
5.1 Differentiating Between Healthy and Unhealthy Fats
- Identifying Sources of Monounsaturated and Polyunsaturated Fats
- Minimizing Saturated and Trans Fats in Your Cart
5.2 Optimal Cooking Oils and Their Culinary Applications
- High Smoke Point Oils for Cooking
- Utilizing Olive Oil and Avocado Oil for Dressings and Flavor

CHAPTER 6: DAIRY AND Dairy Alternatives: Supporting Bone Health

6.1 Nutritional Considerations for Dairy Products

- Choosing Low-Fat and Unsweetened Options

- Incorporating Dairy Alternatives for Lactose Intolerance or Dietary Preferences

6.2 The Importance of Calcium and Vitamin D in Your Cart

- Meeting Daily Calcium Requirements

- Understanding the Role of Vitamin D for Calcium Absorption

CHAPTER 7: MINDFUL Choices in the Snack Aisle

7.1 Navigating the Snack Aisle for Balanced Options

- Identifying Healthy Snack Alternatives

- Managing Portion Sizes for Snacking

7.2 Addressing the Temptation of Processed and Sugary Snacks

- Making Conscious Choices to Limit Processed Foods

- Strategies for Reducing Added Sugar Intake

CHAPTER 8: BEVERAGES: Hydration and Nutrient Considerations

8.1 The Impact of Beverage Choices on Overall Health

- Prioritizing Water and Herbal Teas for Hydration

- Limiting Sugary and Caloric Beverages

8.2 Exploring Nutrient-Rich Beverage Alternatives

- Incorporating Unsweetened Nut Milks and Fruit Infusions

- Making Informed Decisions in the Coffee and Tea Aisles

CHAPTER 9: ETHICAL and Sustainable Choices in the Grocery Store

9.1 Recognizing Labels and Certifications for Ethical Practices

- Understanding the Meaning Behind Labels such as Fair Trade and Rainforest Alliance

- Making Sustainable Seafood Choices

9.2 Supporting Local Farmers and Sustainable Agriculture

- Exploring Farmers' Markets and Local Produce

- Minimizing Environmental Impact Through Informed Choices

CHAPTER 10: BUDGET-Friendly Strategies for Healthier Choices

10.1 Making Nutrient-Dense Choices Within Budget Constraints

- Prioritizing Staples That Offer Maximum Nutritional Value

- Exploring Affordable Protein Sources and Seasonal Produce

10.2 Utilizing Coupons, Sales, and Bulk Purchases

- Maximizing Savings Without Compromising Nutrition

- Planning Meals Based on Cost-Effective Ingredients

CHAPTER 11: MANAGING Impulse Buys and Emotional Eating Triggers

11.1 Strategies for Resisting Impulse Buys and Marketing Tactics

- Creating a Shopping Plan and Sticking to It

- Recognizing Emotional Triggers for Unhealthy Choices

11.2 Mindful Eating Practices to Enhance the Shopping Experience

- Practicing Intuitive Eating and Mindful Decision-Making

- Turning Grocery Shopping into a Positive and Health-Promoting Ritual

CONCLUSION: A HOLISTIC Approach to Health Through Informed Shopping

In conclusion, "Navigating the Aisles" is a comprehensive guide designed to transform grocery shopping into a positive and health-promoting experience. By understanding the key elements of informed choices

Chapter 4

Meal Planning for CKD

Balancing Nutrients for Optimal Kidney Support

HARMONIZING WELLNESS: Balancing Nutrients for Optimal Kidney Support

In the intricate dance of health, the role of nutrition becomes particularly paramount when it comes to supporting optimal kidney function. This exploration dives deep into the art and science of balancing nutrients, providing a comprehensive guide to empower individuals in fostering kidney health through informed dietary choices.

CHAPTER 1: THE SYMPHONY of Nutrition and Kidney Health
    1.1 Unveiling the Interplay Between Diet and Renal Function
    - The Crucial Role of Kidneys in Nutrient Balance
    - How Dietary Choices Can Impact Kidney Health
    1.2 The Importance of a Balanced Diet for Optimal Kidney Support
    - Recognizing the Significance of Balanced Nutrients
    - Navigating the Nuances of Individual Dietary Needs

CHAPTER 2: PROTEIN: The Backbone of Renal Nutrition
    2.1 Understanding Protein's Role in Kidney Function
    - The Essential Functions of Protein in the Body

- Navigating Protein Intake Based on Different Stages of Kidney Disease
2.2 The Delicate Balance: Protein Moderation in Kidney Health
- Addressing Protein-Energy Wasting in Advanced CKD
- High-Quality Protein Sources for Optimal Nutritional Support

CHAPTER 3: CARBOHYDRATES: Fueling Kidney Health with Smart Choices
3.1 The Impact of Carbohydrates on Blood Sugar and Kidneys
- Choosing the Right Type of Carbohydrates for Kidney Health
- Navigating Carbohydrates in the Context of Diabetes and CKD
3.2 Fiber: A Crucial Player in Kidney-Friendly Carbohydrates
- The Role of Dietary Fiber in Renal Function
- Incorporating Fiber-Rich Choices for Sustained Energy

CHAPTER 4: FATS: CRAFTING a Heart-Healthy Nutrient Profile
4.1 The Dichotomy of Fats and Kidney Health
- The Importance of Essential Fatty Acids
- Saturated vs. Unsaturated Fats: Making Informed Choices
4.2 Omega-3 Fatty Acids: A Nutritional Ally for Kidneys
- Exploring the Renal Benefits of Omega-3s
- Choosing Heart-Healthy Cooking Oils for Optimal Nutrition

CHAPTER 5: MICRONUTRIENTS: The Vital Orchestra of Vitamins and Minerals
5.1 The Micronutrient Landscape in Kidney Health
- Essential Vitamins for Renal Function
- The Role of Minerals in Electrolyte Balance
5.2 Phosphorus and Potassium: Micronutrients with Renal Significance

- Managing Phosphorus Intake Through Dietary Choices
- Balancing Potassium Levels for Optimal Kidney Support

CHAPTER 6: SODIUM AND Fluid Balance: Navigating the Ebb and Flow
6.1 The Crucial Role of Sodium in Fluid Regulation
- Understanding Sodium's Impact on Kidney Function
- The Connection Between Sodium and Blood Pressure
6.2 Hydration Strategies: The Art of Fluid Balance
- The Importance of Adequate Hydration in Kidney Health
- Practical Tips for Managing Fluid Intake

CHAPTER 7: CRAFTING Kidney-Friendly Meals: A Nutritional Masterpiece
7.1 Breakfast Choices for Kidney Health
- Nutrient-Dense Morning Options for Optimal Renal Support
- The Importance of a Well-Balanced Breakfast
7.2 Lunch, Dinner, and Snacking Strategies for Kidney Wellness
- Building Balanced Meals Throughout the Day
- Snack Ideas Aligned with Kidney-Friendly Nutrition

CHAPTER 8: COOKING Techniques for Nutrient Preservation
8.1 Low Sodium and Low Phosphorus Cooking Tips
- Enhancing Flavor Without Compromising Health
- The Art of Using Herbs and Spices in Kidney-Friendly Cooking
8.2 Maximizing Flavor Without Sacrificing Nutrition
- Culinary Techniques for Retaining Nutrient Value
- Meal Planning for Variety and Balanced Nutrition

CHAPTER 9: DINING OUT with Kidney Health in Mind

9.1 Navigating Restaurant Menus for Renal Support
- Communicating Dietary Needs to Restaurant Staff
- Making Informed Choices When Eating Out
9.2 Social Situations and Gatherings: Strategies for Kidney-Friendly Dining
- Celebrating Special Occasions Mindfully
- Navigating Social Events While Adhering to Nutritional Guidelines

CHAPTER 10: THE EVOLVING Landscape of Nutrition Research in Kidney Health

10.1 Current Research Trends in CKD Nutrition
- Innovations in Nutritional Approaches
- Potential Breakthroughs on the Horizon
10.2 Integrating Technology in Renal Dietary Management
- Apps and Tools for Nutrient Tracking
- Wearable Devices and Remote Monitoring in Kidney Nutrition.

Sample Meal Plans for Various CKD Stages

NOURISHING THE KIDNEYS: Sample Meal Plans for Various CKD Stages

Embarking on a journey towards kidney health involves not only understanding the nutritional requirements but also translating that knowledge into practical, everyday choices. This comprehensive guide offers sample meal plans tailored to different stages of Chronic Kidney Disease (CKD), providing a roadmap for individuals seeking to nourish their kidneys through thoughtfully crafted and delicious meals.

CHAPTER 1: INTRODUCTION to Kidney-Friendly Meal Planning

1.1 The Role of Nutrition in CKD Management

- Understanding Dietary Guidelines for Kidney Health

- Tailoring Meal Plans to Individual CKD Stages

1.2 The Importance of Balanced Nutrition in CKD

- The Impact of Diet on Kidney Function

- Crafting Meal Plans to Support Overall Well-being

CHAPTER 2: MEAL PLANNING Considerations for CKD Stages 1-2

2.1 Dietary Strategies for Early Stages of CKD

- Emphasizing Balanced Nutrition and Whole Foods

- Incorporating Kidney-Friendly Ingredients in Daily Meals

2.2 Sample Meal Plans for CKD Stages 1-2

- Breakfast, Lunch, and Dinner Ideas

- Snack Options Aligned with Nutritional Guidelines

CHAPTER 3: NAVIGATING Nutrition in CKD Stages 3-4

3.1 Adjustments in Nutritional Focus for Moderate CKD

- Managing Protein and Phosphorus Intake

- Addressing Sodium and Fluid Balance

3.2 Sample Meal Plans for CKD Stages 3-4

- Diverse and Flavorful Recipes for Daily Meals

- Dessert and Treat Options with Kidney Health in Mind

CHAPTER 4: TAILORING Nutrition for Advanced CKD (Stages 5) and Dialysis

4.1 Nutritional Challenges in Advanced CKD and Dialysis

- The Impact of Kidney Function Decline on Nutrient Management

- Special Considerations for Individuals on Dialysis
4.2 Sample Meal Plans for CKD Stage 5 and Dialysis
- Nutrient-Dense Recipes to Support Comprehensive Health
- Adapting Meal Plans to Dialysis Schedules and Dietary Restrictions

CHAPTER 5: PLANT-BASED and Vegetarian Meal Plans for Kidney Health
5.1 Exploring Plant-Based Nutrition for Kidney Support
- The Benefits of a Plant-Centric Approach in CKD
- Incorporating Plant-Based Proteins in Daily Meals
5.2 Sample Plant-Based Meal Plans for Different CKD Stages
- Delicious and Wholesome Plant-Based Recipes
- Ensuring Nutrient Sufficiency in Plant-Driven Diets

CHAPTER 6: CULINARY Tips and Cooking Techniques for Kidney-Friendly Meals
6.1 Enhancing Flavor Without Sacrificing Nutritional Integrity
- The Art of Herbs and Spices in Kidney-Friendly Cooking
- Utilizing Healthy Fats for Culinary Excellence
6.2 Creative Cooking for CKD: Mastering the Basics
- Simple Cooking Techniques to Preserve Nutrient Value
- Adapting Familiar Recipes to Align with Kidney-Friendly Guidelines

CHAPTER 7: THE ROLE of Hydration in Kidney Health: Beverage Ideas
7.1 The Importance of Hydration in CKD Management
- Balancing Fluid Intake Based on Individual Needs
- Hydrating with Kidney-Friendly Beverages
7.2 Sample Beverage Ideas for Optimal Kidney Support
- Infused Water Recipes for Flavorful Hydration

- Choosing Beverages That Align with Dietary Restrictions

CHAPTER 8: DINING OUT with Kidney Health in Mind: Practical Strategies

8.1 Navigating Restaurant Menus for Renal Support
- Communicating Dietary Needs to Restaurant Staff
- Making Informed Choices When Eating Out

8.2 Social Situations and Gatherings: Strategies for Kidney-Friendly Dining
- Celebrating Special Occasions Mindfully
- Navigating Social Events While Adhering to Nutritional Guidelines

CONCLUSION: EMPOWERING Through Culinary Choices

In conclusion, "Nourishing the Kidneys" aims to empower individuals on their journey to kidney health by offering practical and delicious sample meal plans tailored to different stages of CKD. Each chapter unfolds a palette of flavors, providing not just nourishment but also enjoyment on the path to optimal kidney support. May this guide serve as a source of inspiration and culinary delight, making every meal a step toward enhanced well-being.

Chapter 5

Cooking Techniques for Kidney-Friendly Meals

Low Sodium and Low Phosphorus Cooking Tips

Culinary Mastery: Low Sodium and Low Phosphorus Cooking Tips
Embarking on a journey to create delicious and health-conscious meals while managing low sodium and low phosphorus dietary needs requires a unique blend of creativity and culinary wisdom. In this guide, we delve into practical and expert-driven cooking tips tailored to those navigating restricted sodium and phosphorus intake, ensuring that every meal remains a flavorful and nourishing experience.

CHAPTER 1: UNDERSTANDING the Impact of Low Sodium and Low Phosphorus Diets
1.1 The Connection Between Sodium and Phosphorus in the Diet
- Unraveling the Relationship Between Sodium and Phosphorus
- The Role of Low Sodium and Low Phosphorus Diets in Health Management
1.2 Health Implications of High Sodium and Phosphorus Intake
- The Impact on Kidney Health and Cardiovascular Function
- Common Medical Conditions Requiring Sodium and Phosphorus Restriction

CHAPTER 2: LOW SODIUM Cooking Essentials: Flavor Without Compromise
2.1 The Art of Flavor Enhancement in Low Sodium Cooking

- Exploring Herbs and Spices as Flavorful Alternatives
- Techniques for Extracting Maximum Flavor Without Excessive Salt
2.2 Practical Tips for Reducing Sodium Without Sacrificing Taste
- Choosing Fresh Ingredients for Natural Flavors
- Incorporating Umami-Rich Foods for Depth and Sensation

CHAPTER 3: PHOSPHORUS Management: A Culinary Approach
3.1 Phosphorus in Everyday Foods and Its Impact on Health
- Identifying High-Phosphorus Foods in the Diet
- Strategies for Limiting Phosphorus Absorption in the Body
3.2 Low Phosphorus Ingredient Substitutions and Alternatives
- Selecting Phosphorus-Friendly Ingredients for Balanced Nutrition
- Adapting Traditional Recipes to Reduce Phosphorus Content

CHAPTER 4: MASTERING Low Sodium and Low Phosphorus Meal Planning
4.1 Creating Well-Balanced Low Sodium and Low Phosphorus Meals
- Building Meals Around Fresh Produce and Lean Proteins
- Crafting Meal Plans for Varied Nutritional Needs
4.2 Sample Meal Ideas for Different Occasions
- Breakfast, Lunch, Dinner, and Snack Options
- Ensuring Dietary Variety While Adhering to Sodium and Phosphorus Guidelines

CHAPTER 5: SODIUM AND Phosphorus Content in Processed Foods: A Consumer's Guide
5.1 Reading Food Labels for Sodium and Phosphorus Awareness
- Understanding Sodium and Phosphorus Terminology on Labels

- Identifying Hidden Sources of Sodium and Phosphorus in Packaged Foods

5.2 Making Informed Choices in the Grocery Store
- Opting for Low-Sodium and Low-Phosphorus Alternatives
- Reducing Processed Food Intake for Better Dietary Control

CHAPTER 6: COOKING Techniques for Low Sodium and Low Phosphorus Meals

6.1 Low Sodium and Low Phosphorus Cooking Methods
- Grilling, Roasting, and Sautéing for Enhanced Flavors
- Boiling Techniques to Reduce Sodium and Phosphorus Content

6.2 Preserving Nutrients and Flavors Through Cooking Techniques
- Steaming and Baking for Retained Nutritional Value
- Incorporating Broths and Stocks Without Excessive Sodium

CHAPTER 7: BAKING AND Dessert Delights with Low Sodium and Low Phosphorus Focus

7.1 Exploring Low Sodium and Low Phosphorus Sweeteners
- Utilizing Natural Sweeteners in Baking
- Managing Phosphorus in Dessert Recipes

7.2 Delectable Low Sodium and Low Phosphorus Dessert Recipes
- Satisfying Sweet Tooth Cravings Without Compromising Health
- Creating Guilt-Free Indulgences with Thoughtful Ingredients

CHAPTER 8: EATING OUT and Social Situations: Navigating Low Sodium and Low Phosphorus Dining

8.1 Communicating Dietary Needs in Restaurants
- Advocating for Low Sodium and Low Phosphorus Options

- Selecting Restaurants with Health-Conscious Menus

8.2 Strategies for Low Sodium and Low Phosphorus Choices in Social Gatherings

- Bringing Potluck Dishes Aligned with Dietary Restrictions
- Celebrating Occasions Mindfully with Dietary Considerations

CONCLUSION: A CULINARY Adventure in Health

In conclusion, "Culinary Mastery" is more than a guide; it's a culinary adventure that invites individuals to explore the art of low sodium and low phosphorus cooking. With practical tips, delicious recipes, and thoughtful strategies, this guide empowers readers to take charge of their health while savoring the joy of flavorful meals. May this journey into the world of culinary mastery inspire and elevate the dining experience, proving that health-conscious choices can indeed be a delectable delight.

Maximizing Flavor without Compromising Health

MASTERING THE ART: Maximizing Flavor without Compromising Health

In the realm of culinary excellence, the harmonious balance between flavor and health is an art form. This guide embarks on a flavorful journey, unveiling techniques and insights to elevate the taste of your meals while preserving nutritional integrity. Discover the secrets of maximizing flavor without compromising health and indulge in a culinary experience that nourishes both the palate and the body.

CHAPTER 1: THE SYMBIOSIS of Flavor and Health

1.1 Understanding the Interplay Between Taste and Nutrient-Rich Foods

- Exploring the Connection Between Flavorful Ingredients and Health Benefits

- The Psychological Impact of Flavor on Dietary Satisfaction

1.2 The Importance of Balanced Nutrition in Flavorful Cooking

- Navigating the Intersection of Health-Conscious Choices and Culinary Delight

- Crafting Meals That Satisfy Taste Buds and Nutritional Needs

CHAPTER 2: FLAVORFUL Foundations: Herbs and Spices Unveiled

2.1 Elevating Dishes with the Symphony of Herbs and Spices

- Understanding the Unique Profiles of Common Culinary Herbs

- The Art of Blending Spices for Depth and Complexity

2.2 Harnessing the Power of Aromatics and Seasonings

- Infusing Aroma into Cooking for an Enhanced Dining Experience

- Utilizing Fresh and Dried Herbs for Maximum Flavor Impact

CHAPTER 3: CULINARY Alchemy: Balancing Sweet, Sour, Bitter, and Umami

3.1 The Magic of Flavor Balancing in Culinary Creations

- Achieving Harmony Through the Four Primary Tastes

- Incorporating Umami for a Rich and Satisfying Flavor Profile

3.2 Enhancing Dishes with Natural Sweetness and Acidity

- The Art of Balancing Sweet and Sour Notes in Cooking

- Leveraging Bitter Components for Depth and Complexity

CHAPTER 4: HEALTHY Fats: A Culinary Elixir for Flavor

    4.1 Navigating the World of Healthy Fats for Culinary Excellence

    - The Role of Monounsaturated and Polyunsaturated Fats in Cooking

    - Cooking Techniques to Preserve the Integrity of Healthy Fats

    4.2 Enhancing Flavor with Nutrient-Dense Oils and Ingredients

    - Selecting Quality Cooking Oils for Optimal Flavor and Health Benefits

    - Incorporating Nuts, Seeds, and Avocado for Richness and Nutritional Value

CHAPTER 5: FRESH AND Seasonal: A Flavorful Affair with Produce

    5.1 Celebrating the Bounty of Fresh Produce for Maximum Flavor

    - The Impact of Seasonality on Flavorful Cooking

    - Selecting and Storing Fresh Fruits and Vegetables for Peak Flavor

    5.2 Culinary Creativity with Vegetables and Fruits

    - Unique Cooking Methods to Enhance Produce Flavors

    - Incorporating Fruits into Savory Dishes for Unexpected Delight

CHAPTER 6: SMART COOKING Techniques for Maximum Flavor Extraction

    6.1 Searing, Roasting, and Grilling: Techniques for Intense Flavor

    - Achieving Caramelization and Maillard Reaction for Depth

    - Balancing Cooking Techniques for Optimal Results

    6.2 Slow Cooking and Infusion: Extracting Flavor Gradually

    - The Art of Slow Cooking for Infused Flavors

    - Using Broths, Stocks, and Marinades for Subtle and Layered Tastes

CHAPTER 7: GLOBAL INSPIRATIONS: Flavorful Cuisines from Around the World

7.1 Exploring Flavorful Traditions from Various Culinary Regions
- Mediterranean Delights: Olive Oil, Herbs, and Bold Flavors
- Asian Influences: Umami, Soy, and Aromatic Spices
7.2 Fusion Cuisine: Blending Culinary Cultures for Unique Flavors
- Creative Pairings and Combinations for Culinary Innovation
- Global Ingredients for an Eclectic Flavor Palette

CHAPTER 8: MINDFUL Eating: Savoring Each Flavorful Bite

8.1 The Art of Mindful Dining for Enhanced Flavor Perception
- Cultivating Awareness of Taste and Texture
- Strategies for Mindful Eating to Enhance Flavor Appreciation
8.2 Creating Culinary Experiences: Pairing Food with Atmosphere
- The Impact of Surroundings on Flavor Perception
- Designing Memorable Dining Experiences with Thoughtful Considerations

CONCLUSION: A CULINARY Symphony of Flavorful Health

In conclusion, "Mastering the Art" is an invitation to embark on a culinary symphony where flavor and health intertwine seamlessly. Through understanding the nuances of herbs, spices, balancing tastes, and embracing healthy fats, this guide empowers individuals to savor the richness of each bite without compromising nutritional well-being. May your culinary journey be an exploration of taste, a celebration of health, and a testament to the exquisite balance between flavor and vitality.

Chapter 6

Kidney-Approved Recipes

Breakfast

MORNING NOURISHMENT: Crafting a Wholesome Breakfast

Unlocking the potential of a day often begins with the ritual of breakfast—a meal that sets the tone for energy, focus, and vitality. In this exploration of the first meal of the day, we delve into the nuances of breakfast, dissecting its importance, debunking myths, and providing a spectrum of nutritious options for individuals of all walks of life.

CHAPTER 1: THE SIGNIFICANCE of Breakfast in Daily Well-being

   1.1 Understanding the Role of Breakfast in Nutritional Balance

   - Breakfast as the Foundation for Daily Energy

   - Impact on Cognitive Function, Mood, and Overall Health

   1.2 Busting Breakfast Myths: Separating Fact from Fiction

   - Debunking Common Misconceptions About Breakfast

   - Clarifying the Relationship Between Breakfast and Weight Management

CHAPTER 2: THE NUTRITIONAL Essentials: Components of a Balanced Breakfast

   2.1 The Importance of Macronutrients in Morning Fuel

   - Balancing Proteins, Carbohydrates, and Healthy Fats

- Choosing Whole Foods for Sustained Energy Release
2.2 Micronutrients for Morning Vitality
- Incorporating Vitamins and Minerals for Optimal Health
- Exploring the Role of Fiber in Digestive Wellness

CHAPTER 3: BREAKFAST for Different Dietary Preferences and Lifestyles
3.1 Catering to Diverse Dietary Needs
- Breakfast Ideas for Vegetarians and Vegans
- Addressing Gluten-Free and Dairy-Free Options
3.2 Balancing Breakfast for Busy Lifestyles
- Quick and Nutrient-Dense Options for On-the-Go Mornings
- Meal Prepping Strategies for Effortless Breakfasts

CHAPTER 4: CREATIVE and Nutrient-Rich Breakfast Recipes
4.1 Wholesome Breakfasts for Every Palate
- Delicious and Nutritious Smoothie Bowls
- Overnight Oats: A Versatile Canvas for Flavor and Health
4.2 Savory and Protein-Packed Options
- Egg-Based Dishes for Sustained Morning Energy
- Incorporating Lean Proteins into Breakfast for Muscle Support

CHAPTER 5: THE CULTURAL Tapestry of Breakfast Around the World
5.1 Exploring Global Breakfast Traditions
- Traditional Asian Breakfasts: Rice, Noodles, and Dim Sum
- European Breakfast Delights: Pastries, Cheeses, and Cold Cuts
5.2 Fusion Flavors: Blending Culinary Cultures in the Morning
- Creative Cross-Cultural Breakfast Ideas
- Adapting International Favorites for Local Ingredients

CHAPTER 6: BREAKFAST for Specific Health Goals and Conditions

6.1 Tailoring Breakfast for Weight Management
- Protein-Packed Options to Support Satiety
- Balancing Carbohydrates for Steady Blood Sugar Levels

6.2 Heart-Healthy Breakfasts for Cardiovascular Wellness
- Incorporating Omega-3 Fatty Acids and Antioxidants
- Managing Cholesterol Through Nutrient-Dense Choices

CHAPTER 7: BREAKFAST for Kids: Nourishing Young Minds and Bodies

7.1 Meeting Children's Nutritional Needs in the Morning
- Encouraging Healthy Eating Habits from a Young Age
- Kid-Friendly Recipes That Combine Fun and Nutrition

7.2 Addressing Breakfast Challenges for Picky Eaters
- Strategies for Introducing Variety to Kids' Breakfasts
- Creative Approaches to Make Breakfast Appealing to Children

CHAPTER 8: THE RITUAL of Breakfast: Mindful Eating for Well-being

8.1 The Art of Mindful Breakfasts
- Cultivating Presence in Morning Eating Habits
- Building a Connection Between Food and Mindfulness

8.2 Breakfast as a Source of Joy: Creating Positive Morning Habits
- Incorporating Morning Routines for Holistic Wellness
- Celebrating the Ritual of Breakfast as a Daily Affirmation

CONCLUSION: A SYMPHONY of Morning Delight

In conclusion, "Morning Nourishment" serves as a guide to transform breakfast into a daily symphony of flavors, nutrients, and well-being. From understanding its importance to embracing diverse recipes and cultural influences, this exploration aims to inspire individuals to approach breakfast as a celebration of life's vibrant possibilities. May your mornings be filled with nourishment, joy, and the delightful anticipation of a new day's journey.

Lunch

THE ART OF MIDDAY SUSTENANCE: Crafting a Nourishing Lunch

In the bustling tapestry of our daily lives, lunch emerges as a pivotal moment—an opportunity to refuel, rejuvenate, and savor a culinary interlude. This exploration of the midday meal ventures beyond mere sustenance, delving into the intricacies of crafting a lunch that not only satisfies the palate but also nurtures the body and mind.

CHAPTER 1: UNVEILING the Significance of Lunch in Daily Nutrition
    1.1 The Role of Lunch in Maintaining Energy Levels
    - Understanding the Importance of Midday Nourishment
    - Balancing Nutrients to Support Afternoon Productivity
    1.2 The Psychological Impact of a Wholesome Lunch
    - Lunch as a Catalyst for Mental Clarity and Focus
    - The Connection Between Nutrient-Rich Meals and Mood Enhancement

CHAPTER 2: NUTRIENT-Rich Components of a Balanced Lunch
    2.1 Essential Macronutrients for Midday Sustenance
    - Incorporating Lean Proteins for Muscle Support
    - Balancing Carbohydrates to Avoid Afternoon Slumps
    2.2 Micronutrients: The Vital Palette of Vitamins and Minerals

- The Role of Vegetables and Fruits in Lunchtime Nutrition
- Selecting Whole Grains for Sustained Energy Release

CHAPTER 3: TAILORING Lunch for Dietary Preferences and Specialized Diets
3.1 Vegetarian and Vegan Lunch Options for Plant-Powered Nutrition
- Protein-Rich Plant-Based Alternatives
- Creative and Flavorful Meatless Lunch Ideas
3.2 Addressing Gluten-Free, Dairy-Free, and Low-Carb Lunch Variations
- Crafting Lunches for Individuals with Dietary Sensitivities
- Exploring Low-Carb Options for Balanced Nutrition

CHAPTER 4: CREATIVE and Wholesome Lunch Recipes for Every Palate
4.1 Quick and Nutrient-Dense Lunch Options for Busy Days
- Simple Salad Ideas Bursting with Flavor and Nutrients
- Incorporating Superfoods for an Extra Boost
4.2 Hearty and Satisfying Lunches for a Fulfilling Midday Break
- Protein-Packed Grain Bowls with Varied Textures
- Warm and Comforting Soups for Nourishment and Hydration

CHAPTER 5: EMBRACING Global Flavors: A Culinary Journey at Noon
5.1 Exploring Cultural Influences on Lunchtime Delights
- Mediterranean Inspirations: Olive Oil, Grains, and Fresh Produce
- Asian Fusion: Noodles, Stir-Fries, and Savory Broths
5.2 Infusing International Elements into Everyday Lunches
- Creative Twists on Classic Dishes from Around the World
- Adapting Authentic Flavors with Local Ingredients

CHAPTER 6: LUNCH FOR Specific Health Goals and Conditions

    6.1 Supporting Weight Management Through Thoughtful Lunch Choices

    - Balancing Calories and Nutrients for Healthy Weight

    - Strategies for Portion Control and Mindful Eating at Noon

    6.2 Heart-Healthy Lunch Options for Cardiovascular Wellness

    - Incorporating Omega-3 Fatty Acids and Antioxidants

    - Reducing Sodium Intake for Heart Health

CHAPTER 7: LUNCHBOX Wonders: Crafting Nutrient-Packed Meals for Work or School

    7.1 Preparing Flavorful and Nutrient-Rich Lunches in Advance

    - Meal Prep Tips for Effortless Lunchtime Solutions

    - Healthy and Portable Options for School or Office

    7.2 Addressing Common Challenges in Packed Lunches

    - Ensuring Food Safety and Freshness in Packed Meals

    - Creative and Varied Options to Keep Lunch Exciting

CHAPTER 8: THE RITUAL of Lunch: Mindful Eating for Well-being

    8.1 Cultivating Mindfulness in Midday Meals

    - The Art of Savoring Each Bite for Enhanced Satisfaction

    - Incorporating Breaks and Mindful Practices for Mental Wellness

    8.2 Creating a Positive Lunchtime Environment

    - Designing Spaces That Encourage Relaxation and Enjoyment

    - Building a Lunchtime Routine That Nurtures Well-being

CONCLUSION: A CULINARY Tapestry of Midday Delights

In conclusion, "The Art of Midday Sustenance" invites readers to embrace lunch as more than a mere intermission but rather as a vital, delightful thread in the fabric of daily nourishment. From understanding its nutritional nuances to exploring global flavors and creative recipes, this guide aims to transform lunchtime into a cherished and healthful experience. May your midday meals be a celebration of vitality, a moment of culinary joy, and a source of sustained well-being.

Dinner

THE CULMINATION OF Daily Nourishment: Crafting a Wholesome Dinner

As the sun descends and the day draws to a close, dinner emerges as the grand finale—an opportunity to savor the flavors of a well-rounded meal that not only satiates hunger but also nourishes the body for the night ahead. In this exploration of the evening repast, we embark on a journey through the art of crafting a wholesome dinner, weaving together culinary wisdom, nutritional insights, and diverse recipes that cater to various tastes and dietary needs.

CHAPTER 1: UNDERSTANDING the Crucial Role of Dinner in Daily Nutrition

1.1 The Significance of Evening Nourishment
- The Role of Dinner in Supporting Overnight Recovery and Repair
- Balancing Macronutrients for Sustained Energy Throughout the Night

1.2 Dinner and the Circadian Rhythm: Aligning Nutrition with the Body's Internal Clock
- The Connection Between Meal Timing and Metabolic Health
- Strategies for Optimizing Nutrition Based on Circadian Rhythms

CHAPTER 2: THE NUTRIENT Symphony: Components of a Balanced Dinner

2.1 The Importance of Protein in Evening Meals
- Supporting Muscle Repair and Growth Through Protein-Rich Choices
- Plant-Based Protein Alternatives for Vegetarian and Vegan Diets

2.2 Complex Carbohydrates and Healthy Fats: Building a Foundation for Dinner
- Incorporating Whole Grains and Fiber for Satiety
- The Role of Omega-3 Fatty Acids in Dinner for Heart Health

CHAPTER 3: DINNER FOR Various Dietary Preferences and Health Goals

3.1 Plant-Powered Dinners for Vegetarians and Vegans
- Creative and Flavorful Meatless Dinner Ideas
- Ensuring Nutrient Adequacy in Plant-Based Diets

3.2 Dinner for Weight Management and Metabolic Health
- Strategies for Portion Control and Mindful Eating at Dinner
- Balancing Macronutrients to Support Weight Goals

CHAPTER 4: CREATIVE and Nutrient-Dense Dinner Recipes for Every Palate

4.1 Quick and Healthy Dinner Options for Busy Evenings
- One-Pan Wonders: Streamlining Dinner Preparation
- Incorporating Superfoods for an Extra Nutritional Boost

4.2 Hearty and Satisfying Dinner Choices for Comfort and Well-being
- Wholesome Casseroles and Stews for Nourishing Evenings
- Flavorful Grain Bowls with a Variety of Textures and Tastes

CHAPTER 5: EMBRACING Global Flavors: A Culinary Expedition in the Evening

5.1 Exploring Culinary Traditions in Dinner Around the World

- Mediterranean Dinner Inspirations: Olive Oil, Grilled Vegetables, and Legumes

- Asian Fusion: Stir-Fries, Curries, and Unique Spice Blends

5.2 Infusing International Elements into Everyday Dinners

- Adapting Authentic Flavors to Local Ingredients

- Creative Cross-Cultural Dinner Ideas for Culinary Exploration

CHAPTER 6: DINNER FOR Specific Health Conditions and Wellness Goals

6.1 Supporting Cardiovascular Health Through Thoughtful Dinner Choices

- Incorporating Heart-Healthy Ingredients and Cooking Methods

- Reducing Sodium Intake for Overall Cardiovascular Wellness

6.2 Dinner for Digestive Health and Sleep Quality

- Fiber-Rich Choices to Support Digestive Regularity

- The Impact of Dinner Choices on Sleep Duration and Quality

CHAPTER 7: THE FAMILY Table: Crafting Nutritious Dinners for All Ages

7.1 Nourishing Dinner Options for Children and Teens

- Ensuring Nutrient Adequacy for Growing Bodies

- Strategies for Encouraging Healthy Eating Habits in Youth

7.2 Family Dinners: Fostering Connection and Well-being

- The Importance of Shared Meals for Family Bonding

- Creative Approaches to Make Dinner Enjoyable for All

CHAPTER 8: THE RITUAL of Dinner: Mindful Eating for Nighttime Wellness

8.1 Embracing the Calmness of Evening Meals

- Mindful Practices for Relaxing Dinners

- Strategies for Reducing Stress and Promoting Digestive Well-being

8.2 Dinner as a Culinary Journey: Celebrating Daily Achievements and Reflection

- Creating a Positive and Reflective Atmosphere during Dinner

- Cultivating Gratitude and Mindfulness in Evening Eating Habits

CONCLUSION: A SYMPHONY of Evening Sustenance

In conclusion, "The Culmination of Daily Nourishment" seeks to elevate dinner from a routine to a culinary symphony—a harmonious blend of flavors, nutrients, and well-being. Whether exploring global tastes, catering to dietary needs, or embracing mindful practices, this guide aims to transform dinner into a daily celebration of life's diverse and delicious possibilities. May your evenings be filled with nourishment, joy, and the satisfaction of a day well-lived.

Snacks and Desserts

INDULGENCE WITH PURPOSE: Crafting Healthful Snacks and Desserts

In the tapestry of daily nourishment, snacks and desserts serve as delightful interludes—moments to savor flavor, satisfy cravings, and infuse joy into our culinary journeys. This exploration ventures beyond mere indulgence, delving into the art of crafting snacks and desserts that not only titillate the taste buds but also contribute to overall well-being. From mindful munching to guilt-free desserts, let's embark on a flavorful odyssey that transcends the ordinary.

CHAPTER 1: THE ROLE of Snacks and Desserts in a Balanced Diet

1.1 Redefining Snacking: A Strategic Approach to Between-Meal Nourishment

- Understanding the Purpose of Snacks in Daily Nutrition
- Balancing Energy Intake for a Sustained and Vibrant Lifestyle

1.2 Desserts as Occasional Pleasures: A Celebration of Flavor and Culinary Joy

- The Psychological Impact of Savoring Sweet Endings
- Strategies for Incorporating Desserts Without Compromising Health Goals

CHAPTER 2: BUILDING a Nutrient-Rich Snacking Foundation

2.1 Smart Snacking: A Symphony of Macro and Micronutrients

- Balancing Protein, Carbohydrates, and Healthy Fats in Snack Choices
- The Role of Fiber in Promoting Satiety and Digestive Health

2.2 Snacking for Specific Dietary Needs and Goals

- Snack Ideas for Vegetarians and Vegans
- Catering to Gluten-Free, Dairy-Free, and Low-Carb Preferences

CHAPTER 3: CREATIVE and Wholesome Snack Recipes for Every Palate

    3.1 Quick and Nutrient-Dense Snack Options for Busy Days

    - Energizing Nut and Seed Mixes for On-the-Go Nourishment

    - Fruit and Yogurt Parfaits: A Perfect Blend of Sweetness and Nutrition

    3.2 Savory and Satisfying Snacks for a Flavorful Experience

    - Homemade Veggie Chips and Dips for Healthy Crunching

    - Innovative Ways to Incorporate Protein-Rich Ingredients in Snacks

CHAPTER 4: THE SWEET Symphony: Desserts with a Healthful Twist

    4.1 Navigating the World of Sweeteners: A Guide to Mindful Dessert Choices

    - Understanding Natural and Artificial Sweeteners

    - Strategies for Reducing Added Sugar in Dessert Recipes

    4.2 Fruitful Indulgences: Harnessing Nature's Sweetness in Desserts

    - Creative Fruit-Based Dessert Ideas for All Ages

    - Balancing Fruit and Nut Flavors for Irresistible Sweet Treats

CHAPTER 5: MINDFUL Snacking and Dessert Enjoyment

    5.1 The Art of Mindful Eating: Savoring Every Bite with Intention

    - Incorporating Mindfulness Practices into Snacking

    - Creating a Tranquil Environment for Dessert Enjoyment

    5.2 Strategies for Portion Control and Smart Choices in Snacking

    - Navigating Emotional Eating and Stress-Induced Snacking

    - Creative Portioning for Dessert Satisfaction without Excess

CHAPTER 6: SNACKS AND Desserts for Various Lifestyles and Occasions

    6.1 Wholesome Choices for Children's Snacking and Dessert

    - Nutrient-Rich Snack Ideas for Growing Bodies

- Crafting Desserts That Appeal to Young Taste Buds
6.2 Elegant and Healthful Desserts for Special Occasions
- Dessert Ideas for Celebrations Without Compromising Health
- Impressively Flavorful Snack Platters for Entertaining

CHAPTER 7: NAVIGATING Commercial Snacks and Dessert Choices
7.1 Reading Labels: A Guide to Making Informed Choices in Packaged Snacks
- Identifying Hidden Sugars and Artificial Additives
- Choosing Healthful Packaged Snacks for Convenience
7.2 Strategies for Making Healthful Dessert Purchases
- Exploring Health-Conscious Dessert Brands and Products
- Incorporating Commercial Desserts Mindfully into the Diet

CHAPTER 8: THE SWEET Finale: Balancing Enjoyment and Well-being
8.1 The Psychology of Desserts: Enhancing Mood and Culinary Pleasure
- Understanding the Emotional Connection to Sweet Treats
- Incorporating Desserts as a Source of Comfort and Joy
8.2 Nourishing the Soul Through Healthful Snacks and Desserts
- Desserts as a Form of Self-Care and Personal Indulgence
- Savoring the Culinary Tapestry of Life with Mindful Snacking

CONCLUSION: A JOURNEY Beyond the Ordinary

In conclusion, "Indulgence with Purpose" invites readers to explore the world of snacks and desserts with a newfound appreciation for both flavor and well-being. Whether crafting nutrient-rich snacks for daily nourishment or savoring healthful desserts with intention, may this guide elevate your

culinary experiences, allowing you to indulge with purpose and relish the sweetness of life.

Chapter 7

Hydration Strategies for CKD

Importance of Adequate Fluid Intake

Hydration Harmony: Unraveling the Crucial Role of Adequate Fluid Intake

In the intricate dance of maintaining optimal health, few partners are as essential as water. Our bodies, marvels of biological engineering, depend on a delicate balance of fluids to support vital functions. Join me on a journey through the rivers and tributaries of hydration science as we explore the profound importance of adequate fluid intake and how it serves as the lifeblood of well-being.

CHAPTER 1: THE FOUNDATION of Life: Understanding the Essence of Hydration

1.1 The Human Body as a Watery Wonderland

- Unveiling the Percentage of Water Composition in the Body

- The Dynamic Role of Water in Biochemical Reactions and Cellular Function

1.2 The Ripple Effect: How Dehydration Impacts Overall Health

- Exploring the Consequences of Dehydration on Physical and Cognitive Functions

- Recognizing the Subtle Signs of Inadequate Hydration

CHAPTER 2: UNMASKING the Myth: Beyond Water as a Simple Thirst Quencher

2.1 The Multifaceted World of Hydrating Beverages

- Tea, Coffee, and Other Non-Alcoholic Options: How They Contribute to Hydration

- Dispelling Myths About Caffeine's Dehydrating Effects

2.2 Hydration in Solid Form: The Moisture-Rich Bounty of Fruits and Vegetables

- The Water Content of Common Foods and Its Contribution to Daily Fluid Intake

- Integrating Hydration Through Nutrient-Rich Dietary Choices

CHAPTER 3: TAILORING Hydration to Individual Needs

3.1 Demystifying Daily Water Requirements

- Factors Influencing Personal Hydration Needs: From Age to Physical Activity

- Customizing Hydration Plans for Varied Lifestyles and Environmental Conditions

3.2 Hydration for Special Populations: Children, Elderly, and Pregnant Individuals

- Addressing Unique Hydration Needs Across Different Life Stages

- Navigating the Nuances of Hydration During Pregnancy and Lactation

CHAPTER 4: THE POWER of Timing: Strategic Hydration Throughout the Day

4.1 Morning Rituals: Kickstarting the Day with Hydration

- The Benefits of Hydrating First Thing in the Morning

- Infusing Morning Beverages with Healthful Elements

4.2 Hydration at Work and Play: Staying Refreshed During Daily Activities

- Strategies for Maintaining Optimal Hydration in Professional and Recreational Settings

- The Role of Hydration in Enhancing Cognitive Performance

CHAPTER 5: DISPELLING Hydration Myths and Misconceptions

5.1 Beyond the 8x8 Rule: Understanding Hydration Beyond Generic Guidelines

- Debunking Common Misconceptions About Daily Water Intake
- The Myth of Overhydration: Navigating the Balance Between Adequacy and Excess

5.2 Electrolytes: The Unsung Heroes of Hydration

- Unveiling the Role of Electrolytes in Maintaining Fluid Balance
- Hydration Strategies for Athletes and Those Engaged in Intense Physical Activities

CHAPTER 6: HYDRATION and Health: Exploring the Impact on Chronic Conditions

6.1 The Nexus Between Hydration and Kidney Health
- How Fluid Intake Influences Kidney Function and Disease Prevention
- Strategies for Hydrating in Accordance with Specific Kidney Conditions
6.2 Hydration and Heart Health: Unraveling the Connection
- The Influence of Fluid Balance on Cardiovascular Function
- Addressing Hydration Considerations for Individuals with Heart Conditions

CHAPTER 7: NAVIGATING Hydration Challenges: Overcoming Barriers to Optimal Intake

7.1 The Psychological Factors Influencing Hydration Habits
- Addressing Emotional and Behavioral Aspects Impacting Hydration Choices
- Overcoming Hydration Roadblocks Through Mindful Practices
7.2 Practical Tips for Enhancing Daily Hydration

- Innovative Hydration Techniques: Infusions, Hydration Apps, and More
- Cultivating a Hydration-Friendly Environment in Everyday Life

CHAPTER 8: FUTURE FRONTIERS: Hydration Science and Evolving Perspectives

8.1 Emerging Research in Hydration Science

- Innovations in Hydration Monitoring Technologies
- The Intersection of Hydration and Gut Health: Exploring the Microbiome Connection

8.2 Global Perspectives on Hydration: Addressing Water Scarcity and Sustainable Practices

- The Intersection of Hydration and Environmental Sustainability
- Addressing Water Scarcity Challenges and Promoting Access to Clean Water Globally

CONCLUSION: SIPPING Towards Optimal Well-being

In the closing pages of "Hydration Harmony," let's toast to the incredible symphony that unfolds when our bodies are in harmony with the elixir of life—water. May this exploration empower you to embrace hydration as a cornerstone of vitality, unlocking the doors to optimal well-being one sip at a time.

Choosing the Right Beverages

SIP SMART: A COMPREHENSIVE Guide to Choosing the Right Beverages

In the vast landscape of beverage choices, navigating the spectrum from hydrating elixirs to indulgent treats can be akin to a journey through a bustling marketplace. Let's embark on a quest to unravel the secrets of selecting beverages that not only tantalize our taste buds but also contribute to our overall well-being.

CHAPTER 1: DECODING the Drink Spectrum

1.1 The Fluid Foundation: Understanding the Importance of Hydration

- Demystifying the Role of Water as the Ultimate Hydrator

- Exploring How Different Beverages Contribute to Daily Fluid Intake

1.2 Beyond Thirst Quenching: Beverages as Nutritional Allies

- The Nutrient Profiles of Various Drinks: Vitamins, Minerals, and Antioxidants

- Crafting a Balanced Beverage Arsenal for Optimal Health

CHAPTER 2: NAVIGATING the Jungle of Sugary Temptations

2.1 The Hidden Sugars: Unveiling the Dangers of Sugary Beverages

- The Impact of Excessive Sugar on Health: From Weight Gain to Chronic Conditions

- Identifying Sneaky Sugars in Popular Beverages and Alternatives

2.2 Sweet Indulgences: Crafting Healthier Versions of Sugary Delights

- DIY Low-Sugar and Sugar-Free Beverage Recipes

- Navigating the Market for Healthier Commercial Alternatives

CHAPTER 3: THE BREW Buzz: Coffee, Tea, and Beyond

3.1 Coffee Culture: The Health Benefits and Potential Pitfalls

- The Antioxidant Riches of Coffee and Its Impact on Mental Alertness

- Addressing Common Concerns About Caffeine Consumption

3.2 Tea Tales: From Green to Herbal, Unraveling the Health Benefits

- Exploring the Healthful Properties of Various Teas

- Herbal Infusions and Tisanes: A Spectrum of Flavorful and Healthful Choices

CHAPTER 4: A SYMPHONY of Fruitful Delights

4.1 Fresh Perspectives: The Vibrant World of Fruit Juices

- The Nutritional Pros and Cons of Fruit Juices

- Juicing at Home: Maximizing Nutrient Retention and Flavor

4.2 Smoothie Sensations: Blending Taste and Nutrition

- Crafting Nutrient-Dense Smoothies for Energy and Vitality

- Exploring Innovative Ingredients for Smoothie Enhancements

CHAPTER 5: THE ALCHEMY of Alcoholic Beverages

5.1 Moderate Enjoyment: The Potential Health Benefits of Alcohol

- Understanding the Role of Alcohol in Heart Health

- Navigating Sensible Drinking Guidelines and Risks

5.2 Crafting Conscious Cocktails: A Guide to Mindful Mixology

- Low-Alcohol and Non-Alcoholic Alternatives for Health-Conscious Celebrations

- Tips for Reducing the Health Impact of Alcoholic Beverages

CHAPTER 6: PLANT-POWERED Elixirs: Exploring Non-Dairy Milk Alternatives

6.1 The Dairy Dilemma: Navigating Health Considerations

- Understanding Lactose Intolerance and Dairy Allergies

- Unraveling the Debate on Dairy's Impact on Bone Health

6.2 Nutty, Creamy, and Plant-Powered: The Rise of Non-Dairy Milks

- Nutritional Profiles of Popular Non-Dairy Alternatives: Almond, Soy, Oat, and More

- Tips for Choosing the Right Non-Dairy Milk Based on Health Goals

CHAPTER 7: WATER WISDOM: Elevating the Mundane to the Marvelous

7.1 The Elixir of Life: Unlocking the Secrets of Hydration

- The Importance of Water for Every Biological Function

- Tips for Enhancing Water Intake Through Infusions, Electrolytes, and Temperature

7.2 Sustainable Sips: The Environmental Impact of Beverage Choices

- How Beverage Choices Contribute to Environmental Sustainability

- Exploring Innovative Packaging and Recycling Practices

CHAPTER 8: THE FUTURE of Beverages: Trends and Innovations

8.1 Sipping into Tomorrow: Emerging Beverage Trends

- The Advent of Functional and Wellness-Boosting Beverages

- How Technology and Science are Shaping the Future of Beverage Consumption

8.2 Empowered Choices: Navigating Labels and Marketing Tactics

- Deciphering Labels for Hidden Ingredients and Marketing Hype

- Strategies for Making Informed and Empowered Beverage Choices

CONCLUSION: CRAFTING Your Beverage Symphony

As we conclude our exploration into the world of beverages, I invite you to embrace the art of mindful consumption. May you navigate the diverse array of drink options with confidence, creating a harmonious symphony that not only delights your palate but also supports your journey towards a healthier and more vibrant life. Cheers to choosing beverages that truly nourish and uplift!

As we conclude our exploration into the world of beverages, I invite you to embrace the art of mindful consumption. May you navigate the diverse array of drink options with confidence, creating a harmonious symphony that not only delights your palate but also supports your journey towards a healthier and more vibrant life. Cheers to choosing beverages that truly nourish and uplift!

Chapter 8

Dining Out with CKD

Navigating Restaurant Menus

Mastering the Art of Dining Out: A Comprehensive Guide to Navigating Restaurant Menus

In the culinary tapestry of restaurant menus, every dish tells a story, and every choice shapes your dining experience. Embark on a journey with me as we unravel the intricacies of navigating restaurant menus, empowering you to make informed and satisfying choices that align with your taste preferences and nutritional goals.

CHAPTER 1: THE MENU Decoded: Understanding Restaurant Jargon

    1.1 Culinary Terminology: A Glossary for the Modern Diner

    - Unraveling the Language of Chefs: From Sous Vide to Chiffonade

    - Navigating Common Menu Phrases to Enhance Ordering Confidence

    1.2 Dietary Labels and Allergen Information: A Diner's Secret Weapon

    - The Rise of Gluten-Free, Vegan, and Paleo Options

    - How Restaurants Communicate Allergen Information to Ensure Diner Safety

CHAPTER 2: FROM AMUSE-Bouche to Dessert: The Culinary Journey Unveiled

    2.1 Appetizers: Whetting Your Appetite with Flavorful Beginnings

    - Exploring Regional and Global Influences on Appetizer Menus

    - Tips for Choosing Appetizers that Complement Your Main Course

2.2 Navigating Main Courses: Deciding Between Classics and Chef Specialties

- How Chefs Craft Signature Dishes to Showcase Culinary Expertise

- Balancing Indulgence and Nutritional Consciousness in Main Course Selection

2.3 The Sweet Finale: Dessert Decisions for Every Sweet Tooth

- Examining the Diversity of Dessert Menus: From Decadent to Light

- Sharing Desserts and Other Strategies for Satisfying Your Sweet Cravings

CHAPTER 3: CRAFTING a Well-Balanced Meal: The Art of Menu Composition

3.1 Building a Balanced Plate: Incorporating Proteins, Carbs, and Greens

- The Role of Proteins: From Seafood to Plant-Based Options

- The Carb Conundrum: Navigating Grains, Pasta, and Starchy Sides

- Elevating Your Plate with Vibrant Greens and Vegetables

3.2 Mindful Choices: Strategies for Health-Conscious Dining

- Balancing Indulgences with Nutrient-Rich Choices

- Tips for Reducing Sodium, Saturated Fat, and Added Sugars in Restaurant Meals

CHAPTER 4: DINING STRATEGIES for Various Dietary Preferences

4.1 Vegetarian and Vegan Dining: Beyond the Salad Bowl

- Exploring the Richness of Vegetarian and Vegan Menus

- Communicating Dietary Preferences to Ensure a Satisfying Dining Experience

4.2 Gluten-Free Dining: Navigating Menus for Celiac-Friendly Options

- Understanding Gluten-Free Preparation and Cross-Contamination Concerns

- Popular Gluten-Free Substitutes and Grains for Diverse Flavors

CHAPTER 5: THE ART of Pairing: Matching Food with Beverages

5.1 Wine and Dine: Pairing Wines with Various Cuisines

- The Basics of Wine Pairing: Red, White, Rosé, and Sparkling

- Strategies for Pairing Wine with Different Flavors and Spice Levels

5.2 Beyond Wine: Exploring Craft Beer, Cocktails, and Non-Alcoholic Options

- Craft Beer and Its Versatility in Complementing Different Dishes

- Non-Alcoholic Mixology: Elevating Your Dining Experience without Spirits

CHAPTER 6: FROM FINE Dining to Street Food: Navigating Diverse Culinary Settings

6.1 The World on a Plate: Exploring Diverse Ethnic Cuisines

- Navigating Menus from Italian Trattorias to Japanese Izakayas

- Tips for Adapting to Different Culinary Customs and Flavors

6.2 Casual and Fast-Casual Dining: Quick Bites without Sacrificing Quality

- Decoding Menus at Fast-Casual Establishments: A Focus on Freshness

- Strategies for Making Healthier Choices in Casual Dining Settings

CHAPTER 7: SPECIAL Occasions and Celebrations: Making Every Meal Memorable

7.1 Romantic Dinners and Date Nights: Setting the Perfect Culinary Scene

- Choosing Dishes with Romantic Appeal and Shared Desserts

- Selecting Wines and Cocktails to Enhance the Romantic Atmosphere

7.2 Celebratory Feasts: Navigating Menus for Birthdays, Anniversaries, and More

- Customizing Group Menus for Celebrations: From Buffets to Prix Fixe

- The Art of Choosing a Signature Dish to Mark Special Occasions

CHAPTER 8: ETIQUETTE and Tipping: Navigating Social Norms in Dining Out
    8.1 Dining Etiquette: A Guide to Polished and Respectful Dining
    - Table Manners and Common Etiquette Practices in Various Cultures
    - Handling Difficult Dining Situations with Grace and Poise
    8.2 The Art of Tipping: Recognizing Exceptional Service
    - Tipping Guidelines and Practices in Different Countries
    - Acknowledging Service Excellence and Leaving a Positive Impression

CONCLUSION: YOUR CULINARY Compass

As we conclude our exploration of navigating restaurant menus, I hope this guide becomes your culinary compass, empowering you to savor each dining experience to the fullest. May your choices be both delectable and deliberate, creating memorable moments in every bite. Bon appétit!

Communicating Dietary Needs to Servers

NAVIGATING THE CULINARY Landscape: Effectively Communicating Dietary Needs

Dining out is not just a mere act of consumption; it's an experience that engages all the senses. However, for individuals with specific dietary needs or preferences, this experience can become a delicate dance of communication. In this comprehensive guide, we'll explore the art of effectively conveying dietary requirements to servers, ensuring a seamless and enjoyable dining experience tailored to your individual needs.

UNDERSTANDING THE IMPORTANCE of Clear Communication

Effective communication is the cornerstone of a positive dining experience, especially when it comes to dietary needs. Whether you're managing food allergies, adhering to a specific diet plan, or simply avoiding certain ingredients, articulating your requirements clearly is essential. This not only ensures your safety but also allows the culinary team to create a dish that aligns with your preferences.

CHAPTER 1: THE LANGUAGE of Dietary Needs

1.1 Decoding Menus: Navigating Ingredients and Allergen Information

- Understanding the language of menus: Unraveling culinary terms and descriptions.

- Identifying allergens and dietary specifications: A guide to menu labels.

1.2 Common Dietary Restrictions: A Closer Look

- Exploring gluten-free, vegetarian, vegan, and other common dietary preferences.

- Tips for spotting allergens and restricted ingredients on the menu.

CHAPTER 2: STRATEGIES for Effective Communication

2.1 Know Your Needs: Building Self-Awareness

- Understanding your dietary needs: Allergies, intolerances, and lifestyle choices.

- Crafting a personalized list of dietary preferences to streamline communication.

2.2 Communicating Clearly with Servers: Dos and Don'ts

- Articulating your needs with confidence and clarity.

- The importance of direct communication in avoiding misunderstandings.

CHAPTER 3: NAVIGATING Different Culinary Settings

3.1 Fine Dining Etiquette: Crafting a Refined Dining Experience

- Communicating with elegance in upscale establishments.

- Understanding how fine dining kitchens accommodate specific requests.

3.2 Casual Dining and Fast Food: Balancing Speed and Precision

- Strategies for effectively communicating in casual and fast-food settings.

- Tips for navigating diverse menus in a time-sensitive environment.

CHAPTER 4: ALLERGIES and Cross-Contamination Concerns

4.1 The Allergy Conundrum: Ensuring Safety in Every Bite

- Identifying common allergens and hidden ingredients.

- Communicating the severity of allergies to kitchen staff for a safe dining experience.

4.2 Cross-Contamination Awareness: Protecting Against Unintended Exposures

- Understanding the risk of cross-contamination in restaurant kitchens.

- Tips for proactive communication to prevent cross-contact.

CHAPTER 5: TURNING Challenges into Opportunities

5.1 Building a Positive Relationship with Servers and Chefs

- Fostering open communication and understanding with restaurant staff.

- Turning challenges into opportunities for culinary creativity and innovation.

5.2 Handling Mistakes Gracefully: Navigating Unexpected Challenges

- Strategies for addressing misunderstandings and mistakes.

- The role of constructive feedback in improving the dining experience for everyone.

CONCLUSION: EMPOWERING Your Culinary Experience

In the intricate dance between diners and chefs, effective communication transforms dietary needs from a potential obstacle into an opportunity for culinary excellence. By mastering the art of expressing your requirements clearly, you not only ensure your safety but also contribute to the growing trend of inclusive and accommodating dining experiences. Let this guide be your companion on the journey to savoring every bite while navigating the diverse landscape of culinary offerings.

Chapter 9

Integrating Exercise into CKD Lifestyle

Benefits of Physical Activity for Kidney Health

Unveiling the Fountain of Health: The Profound Benefits of Physical Activity for Kidney Well-being

In the pursuit of optimal health, the significance of physical activity cannot be overstated. While exercise is often associated with cardiovascular benefits and weight management, its impact on kidney health is a topic that deserves dedicated attention. This comprehensive exploration delves into the myriad benefits of physical activity for kidney health, unraveling the interplay between exercise and the intricate physiology of our renal system.

CHAPTER 1: UNDERSTANDING the Kidneys and Their Vital Role

1.1 The Kidneys Unveiled: Masters of Homeostasis

- An in-depth look at the anatomy and functions of the kidneys.

- Understanding the role of kidneys in maintaining fluid balance, electrolytes, and blood pressure.

1.2 The Link Between Physical Activity and Kidney Function

- Establishing the connection between exercise and renal efficiency.

- How physical activity supports the kidneys in filtering waste and toxins.

CHAPTER 2: NOURISHING the Kidneys Through Exercise

2.1 Blood Flow and Oxygenation: Fueling Renal Vitality

- The impact of aerobic exercise on enhancing blood flow to the kidneys.

- Oxygenation and nutrient delivery: A catalyst for kidney rejuvenation.

2.2 Weight Management and Kidney Health

- Exploring the relationship between obesity, physical activity, and kidney function.

- How exercise aids in weight management and reduces the risk of kidney-related issues.

CHAPTER 3: DETOXIFICATION Through Sweating: The Kidneys' Trusted Ally

3.1 Sweating it Out: Renal Detoxification Mechanisms

- Understanding the role of sweat in eliminating waste products.

- How physical activity enhances the body's natural detoxification processes.

3.2 Hydration and Kidney Function: Finding the Balance

- The importance of staying hydrated during exercise for optimal kidney performance.

- Tips for maintaining a healthy fluid balance during physical activity.

CHAPTER 4: REDUCING the Risk of Kidney Diseases

4.1 Hypertension and Exercise: A Shield for Kidney Health

- The impact of hypertension on kidney function.

- How regular physical activity helps manage blood pressure and reduce the risk of kidney diseases.

4.2 Diabetes, Exercise, and Kidney Protection

- Exploring the connection between diabetes, a major risk factor for kidney disease, and exercise.

- The role of physical activity in preventing and managing diabetic kidney complications.

CHAPTER 5: TAILORING Exercise for Kidney Health

5.1 Finding the Right Balance: Avoiding Overexertion

- Understanding the importance of moderate exercise for kidney health.

- The risks associated with excessive physical activity and their impact on renal function.

5.2 Kidney-Friendly Exercises: A Comprehensive Guide

- Recommendations for kidney-friendly exercises suitable for different fitness levels.

- Incorporating a variety of activities to support overall kidney well-being.

CHAPTER 6: THE MENTAL and Emotional Dimensions of Kidney Health

6.1 Stress Reduction and Its Positive Influence on Kidneys

- The intricate connection between stress, mental well-being, and kidney health.

- How physical activity serves as a potent tool for stress reduction and mental health enhancement.

6.2 Building Resilience Through Exercise: A Holistic Approach

- The holistic benefits of exercise for mind, body, and kidney health.

- Strategies for incorporating mindfulness and mental resilience into your fitness routine.

CHAPTER 7: REALIZING the Long-Term Rewards

7.1 Longevity and Kidney Health: The Enduring Impact of Exercise

- The correlation between a physically active lifestyle and increased lifespan.

- Building a foundation for sustained kidney health through consistent exercise.

7.2 Personalizing Your Fitness Journey for Kidney Wellness

- Tailoring exercise routines to individual preferences and health status.

- Nurturing a lifelong commitment to physical activity for enduring kidney benefits.

CONCLUSION: EMPOWERING Your Journey to Kidney Vitality

As we unravel the profound benefits of physical activity for kidney health, it becomes clear that exercise is not just a means of sculpting the body; it's a powerful elixir for the intricate renal system. Embark on this journey with newfound knowledge and a commitment to nurturing your kidneys through the transformative magic of movement. Let the pages ahead be a guide, empowering you to embrace a life enriched with the enduring benefits of physical activity for kidney well-being.

Safe Exercise Practices for CKD Patients

SAFEGUARDING WELLNESS: A Guide to Safe Exercise Practices for CKD Patients

In the realm of Chronic Kidney Disease (CKD), incorporating safe and effective exercise practices is not only a possibility but a crucial component of holistic well-being. This comprehensive guide aims to unravel the intricacies of safe exercise for CKD patients, providing valuable insights, evidence-based recommendations, and empowering guidance for those navigating the intersection of fitness and kidney health.

CHAPTER 1: THE FOUNDATION of Understanding CKD

1.1 Demystifying Chronic Kidney Disease

- A comprehensive overview of CKD: Causes, stages, and impact on overall health.

- Understanding the unique challenges CKD patients face in maintaining an active lifestyle.

1.2 The Role of Exercise in CKD Management

- How exercise can be a potent tool in managing CKD symptoms and improving quality of life.

- Addressing common misconceptions and fears related to physical activity in CKD patients.

CHAPTER 2: TAILORING Exercise to CKD Stages

2.1 Navigating Different Stages of CKD: A Personalized Approach

- Customizing exercise plans based on the specific stage of CKD.

- Recommendations for patients in early, middle, and late stages, considering individual health variations.

2.2 Cardiovascular Exercise for Renal Health

- The benefits of cardiovascular exercise for CKD patients.

- Safe and effective cardio workouts tailored to different CKD stages.

CHAPTER 3: STRENGTH Training Safely with CKD

3.1 Building Resilience: Strength Training for CKD Patients

- The role of strength training in preserving muscle mass and bone density.

- Adapting strength workouts to suit CKD patients while minimizing the risk of injury.

3.2 Resistance Training Do's and Don'ts

- Safe resistance training practices, emphasizing proper form and technique.

- How to gradually progress in resistance training without straining the kidneys.

CHAPTER 4: FLEXIBILITY and CKD: A Dynamic Duo

4.1 Flexibility Training for CKD Patients

- The importance of flexibility exercises in maintaining joint health.

- Incorporating stretching routines to improve mobility and reduce the risk of musculoskeletal issues.

4.2 Mind-Body Connection: The Role of Yoga

- Exploring the benefits of yoga for CKD patients.

- Gentle yoga poses and practices to enhance flexibility, balance, and mental well-being.

CHAPTER 5: THE CRITICAL Role of Hydration

5.1 Staying Hydrated: The Cornerstone of Safe Exercise

- The impact of proper hydration on kidney health during exercise.

- Practical tips for maintaining adequate fluid intake without overburdening the kidneys.

5.2 Precautions and Warning Signs

- Recognizing warning signs during exercise that require immediate attention.

- Strategies to ensure a safe workout environment and prevent complications.

CHAPTER 6: CRAFTING Individualized Exercise Plans

6.1 Collaborating with Healthcare Professionals

- The importance of consulting healthcare providers before initiating an exercise regimen.

- Building a collaborative approach between patients, doctors, and fitness professionals.

6.2 Customizing Workouts for CKD Patients

- How to tailor exercise plans to individual preferences, limitations, and interests.

- Balancing variety and consistency in workout routines for long-term adherence.

CHAPTER 7: MOTIVATIONAL Strategies for Sustainable Fitness

7.1 Overcoming Challenges: Staying Motivated with CKD

- Addressing common hurdles and obstacles in maintaining an active lifestyle.

- Motivational strategies for sustaining a positive attitude toward exercise.

7.2 Celebrating Progress: The Journey to Wellness

- Recognizing and celebrating small victories in the journey to better health.

- Fostering a mindset that encourages long-term commitment to safe exercise practices.

CONCLUSION: EMPOWERING CKD Patients Through Safe Exercise

As we conclude this comprehensive guide to safe exercise practices for CKD patients, the overarching theme is one of empowerment. Armed with knowledge, personalized strategies, and a collaborative approach to wellness, individuals with CKD can embrace a more active, healthier lifestyle. May this guide serve as a beacon of hope and practical guidance, illuminating the path toward improved kidney health and overall well-being through the transformative power of safe exercise.

Chapter 10

Mindful Eating for Kidney Wellness

Developing Healthy Eating Habits

Mastering the Art of Developing Healthy Eating Habits
Embarking on the journey of developing healthy eating habits is akin to cultivating a garden of well-being for your body and mind. This comprehensive guide delves into the intricate tapestry of nutrition, offering insights, strategies, and practical tips for fostering a relationship with food that nourishes not only the body but also the soul.

CHAPTER 1: FOUNDATIONS of Healthy Eating
    1.1 Understanding Nutritional Basics
    - Unraveling the mysteries of macronutrients and micronutrients.
    - The role of proteins, carbohydrates, fats, vitamins, and minerals in maintaining overall health.
    1.2 Mindful Eating: A Fundamental Approach
    - Cultivating awareness and mindfulness in your eating habits.
    - Strategies to savor and appreciate each bite for improved digestion and satisfaction.

CHAPTER 2: THE ART of Meal Planning
    2.1 Crafting Balanced and Varied Meals
    - Building meals that encompass a spectrum of nutrients.
    - Tailoring meal plans to individual dietary needs and preferences.
    2.2 Portion Control and Moderation

- The significance of portion control in preventing overeating.
- Practical tips for understanding and implementing moderation in daily meals.

CHAPTER 3: NAVIGATING Nutritional Challenges

3.1 Deconstructing Sugar and Salt Intake
- Understanding the impact of excess sugar and salt on health.
- Practical ways to reduce added sugars and sodium in your diet.

3.2 Addressing Emotional Eating
- Unraveling the connection between emotions and eating habits.
- Strategies for breaking free from emotional eating patterns.

CHAPTER 4: EMBRACING Nutrient-Rich Foods

4.1 The Power of Whole Foods
- The benefits of incorporating whole, minimally processed foods.
- Building a colorful plate with a variety of fruits, vegetables, whole grains, and lean proteins.

4.2 Superfoods and Their Contributions
- Exploring the nutritional prowess of superfoods.
- Integrating nutrient-dense options into your daily diet.

CHAPTER 5: SUSTAINABLE and Practical Eating Habits

5.1 Long-Term Sustainability in Healthy Eating
- Strategies for making healthy eating a sustainable lifestyle.
- Navigating social and cultural aspects while maintaining nutritional goals.

5.2 Smart Shopping and Meal Prep
- Tips for efficient grocery shopping and meal preparation.

- How to plan ahead for busy days and reduce reliance on unhealthy convenience foods.

CHAPTER 6: THE MIND-Body Connection in Eating

6.1 The Gut-Brain Axis

- Understanding the intricate relationship between gut health and mental well-being.

- Foods that promote mental clarity, focus, and a positive mood.

6.2 Developing a Healthy Relationship with Food

- Strategies to overcome guilt and anxiety associated with food.

- Fostering a positive and balanced approach to eating.

CHAPTER 7: CULTURAL Considerations in Healthy Eating

7.1 Embracing Cultural Diversity in Nutrition

- Celebrating the richness of diverse dietary traditions.

- How to adapt and integrate cultural influences into a healthy eating framework.

7.2 Navigating Dietary Restrictions and Preferences

- Strategies for individuals with dietary restrictions or preferences.

- Tips for maintaining nutritional balance within specific dietary frameworks.

CONCLUSION: YOUR PERSONAL Journey to Nutritional Mastery

As we conclude this exploration of developing healthy eating habits, it is our sincere hope that this guide serves as a beacon of knowledge and inspiration. The journey to cultivating a nourishing relationship with food is a personal and transformative one. May the insights, strategies, and practical

tips shared empower you on your path to nutritional mastery, fostering a lifetime of wellness and vitality. Remember, every bite is an opportunity to invest in your health and savor the joys of a vibrant and fulfilling life.

The Emotional Connection to Nutrition

UNVEILING THE COMPLEX Tapestry: The Emotional Connection to Nutrition

In the intricate dance of our daily lives, nutrition is more than just fuel for the body; it intertwines with our emotions, shaping not only our physical health but also our mental and emotional well-being. This exploration dives deep into the fascinating realm where food and emotions converge, unraveling the complex interplay between what we consume and how we feel.

CHAPTER 1: FOUNDATIONS of the Mind-Body Bond

1.1 Understanding Emotional Eating

- Exploring the roots of emotional eating behaviors.

- Recognizing the distinction between physical hunger and emotional cravings.

1.2 The Impact of Nutrition on Mood

- Delving into the science of how nutrients influence neurotransmitters.

- Identifying mood-enhancing foods and their effects on emotional well-being.

CHAPTER 2: COMFORT Food and Emotional Resonance

2.1 The Comfort Food Phenomenon

- Analyzing the psychology behind seeking comfort in specific foods.

- Strategies for creating a balanced approach to comfort eating.

2.2 Breaking the Cycle of Emotional Eating

- Practical tips for recognizing and interrupting emotional eating patterns.

- Cultivating healthier coping mechanisms for emotional distress.

CHAPTER 3: STRESS, Cortisol, and Nutritional Harmony

3.1 The Stress-Nutrition Connection

- Understanding the impact of stress on nutritional choices.

- Adapting nutrition strategies to mitigate the effects of stress on the body.

3.2 Mindful Eating as a Stress-Relief Tool

- Incorporating mindfulness practices into mealtime.

- Techniques for breaking the cycle of stress-driven unhealthy eating habits.

CHAPTER 4: THE ROLE of Nutrition in Mental Health

4.1 Nutritional Psychiatry: A New Frontier

- Exploring the emerging field of nutritional psychiatry.

- Foods that support mental health and cognitive function.

4.2 Nutrient Deficiencies and Mental Well-Being

- Identifying common nutrient deficiencies linked to mental health issues.

- Strategies for maintaining optimal nutrient levels for mental wellness.

CHAPTER 5: CULINARY Comforts: Beyond Emotional Eating

5.1 The Art of Mindful Cooking

- Connecting emotionally with the cooking process.

- Crafting meals with intention and mindfulness.

5.2 Food as a Social and Emotional Experience

- Navigating social and cultural aspects of food.

- Balancing the emotional aspects of communal dining.

CHAPTER 6: HEALING Trauma Through Nutrition

6.1 Nutritional Strategies for Trauma Recovery

- Foods that support the healing process after trauma.

- Collaborative approaches integrating nutrition into trauma therapy.

6.2 Mind-Body Practices for Emotional Healing

- The synergy of nutrition and mind-body practices in trauma recovery.

- Building a holistic toolkit for emotional well-being.

CHAPTER 7: CRAFTING a Personalized Emotional Nutrition Plan

7.1 Assessing Individual Emotional Triggers

- Tools for identifying personal emotional triggers related to food.

- Creating a personalized plan for responding to emotional cues.

7.2 Seeking Professional Guidance

- The role of nutritionists, therapists, and counselors in emotional nutrition.

- Forming a collaborative approach to holistic well-being.

CONCLUSION: NOURISHING the Mind and Body Harmony

In concluding this profound exploration of the emotional connection to nutrition, may this guide serve as a compass on your journey toward cultivating a harmonious relationship between your mind and body. Remember, the choices we make in the realm of nutrition are not only about sustenance but also about embracing the rich tapestry of our emotional lives. May your path be illuminated with self-discovery, mindful choices, and a profound understanding of the intricate dance between what you eat and how you feel.

Chapter 11

Monitoring and Managing CKD Progress

Regular Checkups and Lab Tests

Nurturing Wellness: The Essential Guide to Regular Checkups and Lab Tests

In the intricate tapestry of health and well-being, the role of regular checkups and lab tests is akin to the vigilant caretaker ensuring the vitality of the human body. This comprehensive guide delves into the paramount importance of these health evaluations, unraveling the layers of knowledge that empower individuals to take charge of their physical well-being.

CHAPTER 1: THE FOUNDATION of Preventive Health

1.1 Understanding the Essence of Regular Checkups

- Delving into the significance of preventive healthcare.

- The role of early detection in mitigating health risks.

1.2 Decoding Lab Tests: A Diagnostic Symphony

- Unraveling the purpose and types of diagnostic lab tests.

- The synergy between clinical assessments and overall well-being.

CHAPTER 2: THE ART of Scheduling: A Calendar of Health

2.1 Crafting a Personalized Health Calendar

- Guidelines for establishing an individualized checkup schedule.

- The interplay between age, lifestyle, and the frequency of health evaluations.

2.2 Navigating Annual, Biennial, and Specialized Checkups

- The core components of annual checkups.
- The role of biennial checkups and specialized assessments.

CHAPTER 3: BREAKING Down the Components of Regular Checkups
   3.1 Vital Sign Assessments: Beyond the Basics
- Understanding blood pressure, heart rate, and respiratory rate.
- The nuances of interpreting vital signs in different age groups.
   3.2 The Comprehensive Physical Examination
- A step-by-step guide to a thorough physical examination.
- Detecting early signs of potential health issues through physical assessments.

CHAPTER 4: THE LABORATORY Landscape: Key Blood Tests Unveiled
   4.1 Complete Blood Count (CBC): A Window into Health
- Interpreting the components of a CBC and their significance.
- Health conditions identified through abnormalities in blood cell counts.
   4.2 Lipid Profile: Navigating Cholesterol Levels
- Understanding cholesterol levels and their impact on heart health.
- Dietary and lifestyle strategies for maintaining optimal lipid profiles.

CHAPTER 5: METABOLIC Markers and Blood Sugar Dynamics
   5.1 Glucose Levels: Monitoring Sugar Metabolism
- The importance of blood glucose levels in diabetes prevention.
- Lifestyle interventions for stabilizing blood sugar.
   5.2 Assessing Thyroid Function: The Metabolic Regulator
- The role of thyroid hormones in metabolism.
- Interpreting thyroid function test results and potential imbalances.

CHAPTER 6: COMPREHENSIVE Health Panels: Beyond the Basics

6.1 Renal Function Tests: Gauging Kidney Health

- Exploring kidney function indicators and their clinical relevance.
- Dietary and lifestyle factors influencing renal health.

6.2 Liver Function Tests: Nurturing Hepatic Wellness

- Understanding liver enzymes and their diagnostic significance.
- Strategies for promoting liver health through nutrition and lifestyle.

CHAPTER 7: GENETIC and Hormonal Insights

7.1 Genetic Testing: A Glimpse into Personalized Health Risks

- The evolving landscape of genetic testing for health insights.
- Ethical considerations and decision-making around genetic information.

7.2 Hormonal Assessments: Balancing the Endocrine Symphony

- Key hormones affecting overall health and vitality.
- Lifestyle adjustments for hormonal balance and well-being.

CHAPTER 8: RADIOLOGICAL Imaging: A Window to Internal Landscapes

8.1 X-rays, MRIs, and CT Scans: Mapping the Internal Terrain

- The role of imaging studies in diagnostic medicine.
- Understanding when and why different imaging modalities are employed.

8.2 The Importance of Cancer Screenings

- Overview of common cancer screening tests and their significance.
- Early detection strategies for effective cancer prevention.

CHAPTER 9: NAVIGATING Results and Engaging in Health Dialogues

9.1 Interpreting Test Results: From Numbers to Health Insights
- A guide to understanding common health indicators.
- Communicating with healthcare providers about test findings.
9.2 Engaging in Informed Health Discussions
- Strategies for effective communication with healthcare professionals.
- Advocating for personalized and collaborative healthcare.

CONCLUSION: EMPOWERING Health through Knowledge

As we conclude this enlightening journey into the realm of regular checkups and lab tests, may this guide serve as a beacon illuminating the path to proactive health management. Remember, your health is an ongoing narrative, and with the knowledge gleaned from this exploration, you are better equipped to craft a story of well-being, resilience, and vitality. May each checkup be a step towards understanding, each lab test a brushstroke on the canvas of your health journey. Embrace the power of prevention, for in it lies the key to a thriving and resilient life.

Adjusting Your Diet According to CKD Changes

NOURISHING RESILIENCE: Tailoring Your Diet to Navigate Changes in CKD

In the intricate dance of health and well-being, adjusting one's diet according to changes in Chronic Kidney Disease (CKD) becomes a pivotal choreography. This comprehensive guide unfolds the nuances of dietary adaptations, providing a roadmap for individuals navigating the intricate landscape of CKD changes. Your journey toward holistic well-being begins with the understanding that nourishment is a dynamic and personalized endeavor, especially when faced with the challenges presented by CKD.

CHAPTER 1: DECODING Chronic Kidney Disease

1.1 Unveiling the Complexity of CKD

- Exploring the multifaceted nature of Chronic Kidney Disease.

- Understanding the progressive stages and implications for dietary adjustments.

1.2 The Interplay of Diet and CKD Progression

- Unraveling the intricate relationship between nutrition and kidney health.

- Navigating the impact of CKD on dietary requirements.

CHAPTER 2: DIETARY Foundations for Kidney Health

2.1 The Role of Fluid Balance

- Understanding the significance of fluid intake in CKD management.

- Practical tips for maintaining optimal fluid balance.

2.2 The Power of Balanced Nutrition

- Crafting a kidney-friendly diet rich in essential nutrients.

- Balancing macronutrients and micronutrients for kidney support.

CHAPTER 3: TAILORING Protein Intake for Kidney Wellness

    3.1 Protein: Friend or Foe in CKD?

    - Navigating the delicate balance of protein in kidney health.

    - Identifying high-quality protein sources and moderating intake.

    3.2 Proteins to Embrace and Limit

    - A detailed exploration of proteins beneficial for CKD patients.

    - Restricting proteins that may exacerbate kidney concerns.

CHAPTER 4: MANAGING Sodium and Potassium Levels

    4.1 Unmasking the Impact of Sodium in CKD

    - The role of sodium in fluid balance and blood pressure regulation.

    - Strategies for reducing sodium intake without compromising flavor.

    4.2 Potassium: A Delicate Balance

    - Understanding potassium dynamics in CKD.

    - Identifying potassium-rich foods and adopting smart dietary choices.

CHAPTER 5: THE DANCE of Phosphorus and Calcium

    5.1 Phosphorus Management Strategies

    - Exploring the impact of phosphorus on kidney health.

    - Dietary choices to regulate phosphorus levels.

    5.2 Calcium Counterbalance

    - Ensuring adequate calcium intake while managing phosphorus.

    - Optimal sources of dietary calcium for CKD patients.

CHAPTER 6: VITAMINS and Minerals: Allies in Kidney Support

    6.1 Navigating Vitamin D and Kidney Health

- Understanding the intricate relationship between vitamin D and CKD.
- Sunlight, supplements, and dietary sources for vitamin D.

6.2 Micronutrients for Robust Kidney Function
- The role of essential vitamins and minerals in supporting kidney wellness.
- Crafting a diet rich in antioxidants for kidney protection.

CHAPTER 7: SPECIALIZED Diets for CKD

7.1 The Renal Diet: A Tailored Approach
- Defining the renal diet and its customization for CKD stages.
- A detailed exploration of menu planning for renal diets.

7.2 Mediterranean and DASH Diets: Adapting for Kidney Health
- Integrating principles of renowned diets for CKD adjustments.
- Embracing the benefits of Mediterranean and DASH diets.

CHAPTER 8: PRACTICAL Tips for Everyday Eating

8.1 Cooking Strategies for CKD Patients
- Maximizing flavor while adhering to kidney-friendly principles.
- Practical tips for adapting recipes to fit CKD dietary guidelines.

8.2 Dining Out with CKD: A Guide for Savvy Choices
- Navigating restaurant menus and making informed choices.
- Communicating dietary needs to ensure a kidney-friendly dining experience.

CHAPTER 9: NURTURING Emotional Well-being Through Food

9.1 The Emotional Connection to Nutrition
- Acknowledging the psychological aspect of dietary adjustments.
- Strategies for maintaining a positive relationship with food.

9.2 The Role of Support Systems

- Leveraging community and professional support for dietary changes.
- Encouraging emotional resilience on the journey to kidney health.

CONCLUSION: YOUR PERSONALIZED Dietary Odyssey

As we conclude this comprehensive guide, it is our hope that the insights shared will empower you on your unique dietary odyssey through the twists and turns of Chronic Kidney Disease. Remember, nourishing resilience is not a one-size-fits-all endeavor but a personalized journey guided by knowledge, intention, and a deep connection with your well-being. May each dietary choice be a step toward fostering kidney health and embracing a life of vitality and balance.

Chapter 12

Frequently Asked Questions

Common Concerns and Solutions

NAVIGATING COMMON CONCERNS: Expert Solutions for Everyday Challenges

In the realm of health and well-being, common concerns often arise, demanding reliable solutions grounded in expertise. This comprehensive guide addresses prevalent issues faced by individuals of all ages, genders, and backgrounds, providing accurate information and expert-driven solutions. As we embark on this journey through common concerns, our mission is to empower you with knowledge, clarity, and actionable strategies to enhance your overall well-being.

CHAPTER 1: STRESS MANAGEMENT Techniques

1.1 Understanding the Impact of Stress

- Delving into the multifaceted nature of stress on mental and physical health.

- Identifying common stressors in everyday life.

1.2 Mindfulness and Relaxation Practices

- Unveiling the power of mindfulness and relaxation techniques.

- Practical exercises to alleviate stress and foster a sense of calm.

CHAPTER 2: SLEEP HYGIENE for Optimal Rest

2.1 The Importance of Quality Sleep

- Exploring the critical role of sleep in overall health.

- Common sleep-related concerns and their implications.

2.2 Establishing Healthy Sleep Habits

- Practical tips for improving sleep hygiene.

- Creating a conducive sleep environment for restful nights.

CHAPTER 3: NUTRITION Myths and Facts

3.1 Navigating the Landscape of Nutrition

- Dispelling common myths surrounding nutrition.

- Fact-checking popular dietary trends for informed choices.

3.2 Building a Balanced Diet

- Identifying key components of a balanced and nutritious diet.

- Practical steps to achieve optimal nutrition for diverse lifestyles.

CHAPTER 4: FITNESS Fundamentals for Everyone

4.1 Overcoming Barriers to Exercise

- Addressing common obstacles to maintaining a regular fitness routine.

- Tailoring exercise plans to individual needs and preferences.

4.2 Inclusive and Accessible Workouts

- Exploring exercise options for different fitness levels and abilities.

- Fostering a positive and inclusive approach to physical activity.

CHAPTER 5: EFFECTIVE Time Management Strategies

5.1 The Art of Prioritization

- Strategies for effective time management in a fast-paced world.

- Balancing work, personal life, and self-care.

5.2 Maximizing Productivity

- Tools and techniques to boost productivity and minimize procrastination.

- Creating a realistic and sustainable daily routine.

CHAPTER 6: RELATIONSHIPS and Communication Skills

6.1 Nurturing Healthy Connections

- Building and maintaining meaningful relationships.

- Effective communication strategies for enhanced interpersonal connections.

6.2 Resolving Conflict Constructively

- Approaches to resolving conflicts with empathy and understanding.

- Strengthening relationships through effective communication.

CHAPTER 7: FINANCIAL Wellness: From Budgeting to Investments

7.1 Mastering Budgeting Basics

- Creating a practical budget for financial stability.

- Overcoming common financial challenges.

7.2 Investment Strategies for Long-Term Growth

- Introduction to investment options and strategies.

- Building a secure financial future through informed choices.

CHAPTER 8: MENTAL HEALTH Awareness and Coping Strategies

8.1 Breaking the Stigma Around Mental Health

- Promoting mental health awareness and destigmatization.

- Recognizing signs of common mental health concerns.

8.2 Coping Mechanisms and Seeking Support

- Practical coping strategies for managing stress and mental health challenges.

- Encouraging open conversations and seeking professional support.

CONCLUSION: EMPOWERING Your Journey to Well-being

As we conclude this exploration of common concerns and expert solutions, our goal is to leave you equipped with valuable insights and actionable strategies. Remember, well-being is a continuous journey, and every step taken toward self-improvement is a triumph. May the wisdom shared in these pages guide you to a life filled with resilience, balance, and a profound sense of well-being.

Expert Insights on CKD Nutrition

EXPERT INSIGHTS ON CKD Nutrition

Chronic Kidney Disease (CKD) poses unique challenges to individuals, requiring a nuanced approach to nutrition. In this comprehensive exploration, we delve into expert insights on CKD nutrition, providing accurate and actionable information to empower those navigating this health journey. Our goal is to distill the expertise of seasoned professionals into practical guidance that individuals can incorporate into their daily lives.

Chapter 1: Understanding Chronic Kidney Disease

1.1 Introduction to CKD

- Defining Chronic Kidney Disease and its prevalence.

- Exploring the impact of CKD on overall health.

1.2 Stages and Progression

- Detailing the stages of CKD and their implications.

- Understanding the progression and monitoring of the disease.

Chapter 2: The Role of Nutrition in CKD Management

2.1 Nutritional Requirements

- Examining the unique nutritional needs of individuals with CKD.

- Highlighting the importance of personalized nutrition plans.

2.2 Managing Protein Intake

- Balancing protein consumption to support kidney function.

- Identifying high-quality protein sources suitable for CKD patients.

Chapter 3: Controlling Sodium and Fluid Intake

3.1 Sodium's Impact on CKD

- Exploring the relationship between sodium and kidney health.

- Practical tips for reducing sodium intake without compromising flavor.

3.2 Fluid Management

- Understanding the role of fluid balance in CKD.

- Guidelines for optimal fluid intake tailored to individual needs.

Chapter 4: Balancing Electrolytes

4.1 Potassium Management

- Navigating potassium levels in CKD-friendly diets.

- Recognizing foods rich in potassium and making informed choices.

4.2 Phosphorus Considerations

- Addressing the challenges of phosphorus control in CKD.

- Tips for choosing low-phosphorus foods without sacrificing variety.

Chapter 5: Micronutrients and Antioxidants

5.1 Vitamins and Minerals

- Examining the impact of CKD on micronutrient balance.

- Incorporating essential vitamins and minerals through diet and supplementation.

5.2 Antioxidant-Rich Foods

- Harnessing the power of antioxidants to combat oxidative stress.

- Recommendations for antioxidant-rich food choices.

Chapter 6: Meal Planning and Recipes

6.1 Personalized Meal Plans

- Crafting personalized meal plans based on individual CKD stages.

- Adapting dietary recommendations to lifestyle and preferences.

6.2 CKD-Friendly Recipes

- Providing a repertoire of delicious and kidney-friendly recipes.

- Balancing nutrition and flavor in everyday meals.

Chapter 7: Lifestyle Factors and CKD

7.1 Physical Activity

- Exploring the role of exercise in CKD management.

- Tailoring exercise routines to individual capabilities.

7.2 Stress Reduction

- Understanding the impact of stress on CKD.

- Implementing stress reduction techniques for overall well-being.

Conclusion: Empowering Your CKD Nutrition Journey

As we conclude this exploration of expert insights on CKD nutrition, our aim is to empower individuals with knowledge that transcends medical jargon. By distilling complex information into practical advice, we hope to guide you towards a balanced and fulfilling life despite the challenges of Chronic Kidney Disease. Remember, your journey to better health is a continuous process, and with informed choices, you can navigate the path ahead with confidence and resilience.

Chapter 13

Resources and Further Reading

Additional References for In-Depth Knowledge

Additional References for In-Depth Knowledge
To further enrich your understanding of the topics discussed in this book, we have compiled a list of additional references that provide in-depth knowledge on various aspects related to the subject matter. These resources encompass authoritative publications, scientific studies, and reputable organizations that contribute valuable insights to the field. By exploring these references, you can delve deeper into specific areas of interest and gain a more comprehensive grasp of the subject matter.

Chapter 1: Understanding Chronic Kidney Disease

1.1 National Kidney Foundation (NKF) Guidelines

- Access the latest guidelines and recommendations from NKF for managing Chronic Kidney Disease.

1.2 PubMed: Research Articles on CKD

- Explore peer-reviewed research articles on CKD epidemiology, etiology, and progression.

Chapter 2: The Role of Nutrition in CKD Management

2.1 Academy of Nutrition and Dietetics

- Gain insights from the Academy's resources on personalized nutrition plans for individuals with CKD.

2.2 Journal of Renal Nutrition

- Delve into the Journal's articles for in-depth discussions on managing protein intake and nutritional requirements in CKD.

Chapter 3: Controlling Sodium and Fluid Intake

3.1 CDC's Sodium Reduction Resources

- Learn more about sodium reduction strategies from the Centers for Disease Control and Prevention.

3.2 Nephrology Dialysis Transplantation Journal

- Access articles discussing fluid management and its impact on CKD progression.

Chapter 4: Balancing Electrolytes

4.1 American Society of Nephrology (ASN)

- Explore ASN's resources for comprehensive insights into managing potassium and phosphorus levels in CKD.

4.2 Clinical Journal of the American Society of Nephrology

- Refer to this journal for research articles on phosphorus control in chronic kidney disease.

Chapter 5: Micronutrients and Antioxidants

5.1 World Health Organization (WHO) - Micronutrient Information

- Access WHO's information on essential vitamins and minerals, especially relevant for CKD patients.

5.2 The Journal of Nutrition

- Find articles on the role of antioxidants in kidney health in this reputable nutrition journal.

Chapter 6: Meal Planning and Recipes

6.1 Renal Nutrition Forum

- Gain practical meal planning tips and kidney-friendly recipes from this dedicated forum.

6.2 DaVita's Kidney-Friendly Recipes

- Explore a variety of delicious recipes tailored for individuals with kidney concerns.

Chapter 7: Lifestyle Factors and CKD

7.1 American Heart Association (AHA) - Physical Activity Recommendations

- Follow AHA's guidelines on incorporating physical activity into a CKD-friendly lifestyle.

7.2 Mindfulness-Based Stress Reduction (MBSR) Programs

- Learn about stress reduction techniques through MBSR programs to promote overall well-being.

These additional references serve as valuable companions to the information presented in this book. Whether you are a healthcare professional, a patient, or someone with a general interest in kidney health, exploring these resources will enhance your knowledge and contribute to a more nuanced understanding of the complexities associated with Chronic Kidney Disease.

Support Organizations for CKD Patients

SUPPORT ORGANIZATIONS for CKD Patients

Chronic Kidney Disease (CKD) presents a myriad of challenges for individuals and their families. Navigating the complexities of managing CKD often requires more than just medical intervention; it requires a holistic approach that addresses the emotional, social, and informational needs of patients. Support organizations play a pivotal role in providing assistance, resources, and a sense of community for those affected by CKD. In this comprehensive guide, we will explore various support organizations dedicated to empowering CKD patients and fostering a network of understanding and resilience.

Understanding the Role of Support Organizations

Support organizations for CKD patients serve as lifelines, offering a range of services designed to enhance the quality of life for individuals dealing with kidney-related issues. From educational resources to emotional support, these organizations are committed to creating a supportive environment that empowers patients to navigate the challenges of CKD with resilience and knowledge.

1. National Kidney Foundation (NKF)

The National Kidney Foundation is a cornerstone in the CKD support landscape. Renowned for its commitment to preventing kidney diseases and improving the lives of those affected, NKF provides a wealth of resources. These include educational materials, support groups, and access to professionals specializing in kidney health. NKF's comprehensive approach ensures that patients and their families have access to up-to-date information and a supportive community.

2. American Association of Kidney Patients (AAKP)

The American Association of Kidney Patients is a patient-centric organization that strives to improve the quality of life for kidney patients through advocacy, education, and community engagement. AAKP's programs encompass various aspects, including patient education webinars, advocacy efforts for policy change, and opportunities for patients to connect with others facing similar challenges. Their commitment to empowering patients is evident in their multifaceted approach to CKD support.

Nurturing Emotional Well-being

CKD often takes a toll on patients' emotional well-being. Support organizations recognize the importance of addressing these aspects and provide resources that focus on mental health and emotional support.

3. The Renal Support Network (RSN)

The Renal Support Network emphasizes the human side of kidney disease, acknowledging the emotional challenges patients face. RSN offers peer support through its patient-hosted support groups, educational materials, and an annual patient-led conference. By prioritizing emotional well-being, RSN contributes to a holistic approach in managing CKD.

4. Psychosocial Aspects of Chronic Disease (PACD)

PACD, part of the American Psychological Association, delves into the psychosocial aspects of living with chronic diseases, including CKD. Understanding the emotional impact of chronic illness is crucial, and PACD provides resources for patients and their families to navigate these challenges effectively.

Building Community and Connection

Community engagement is a cornerstone of CKD support. Connecting with others who share similar experiences fosters a sense of belonging and understanding.

5. Dialysis Patient Citizens (DPC)

Dialysis Patient Citizens is committed to improving dialysis patients' quality of life through advocacy and education. DPC's initiatives include patient-led webinars, educational resources, and opportunities for patients to engage with policymakers. By fostering a sense of community and empowering patients to be advocates for their own health, DPC contributes to the broader CKD support network.

6. Kidney Community Emergency Response (KCER) Coalition

The KCER Coalition focuses on disaster preparedness and emergency response specific to the kidney community. Ensuring that CKD patients are prepared for emergencies is a critical aspect of support. KCER provides resources and guidance to help individuals with kidney disease navigate emergencies effectively.

Bridging Information Gaps

Understanding the intricacies of CKD and its management is crucial. Support organizations play a pivotal role in disseminating accurate information and bridging knowledge gaps.

7. International Society of Nephrology (ISN) - 0 by 25 Initiative

While ISN is primarily an academic society, its 0 by 25 Initiative highlights the commitment to eliminating preventable deaths from acute kidney injury by 2025. By promoting awareness and education, ISN contributes to the global effort to prevent kidney-related deaths, aligning with the goals of many CKD support organizations.

Conclusion

Support organizations for CKD patients are beacons of hope, guidance, and understanding in the journey of kidney health. By offering a spectrum of services encompassing education, emotional well-being, community building, and information dissemination, these organizations contribute significantly to enhancing the lives of individuals affected by CKD. As we navigate the landscape of CKD support, these organizations serve as pillars of strength, empowering patients to face the challenges of kidney disease with resilience and knowledge.

Conclusion

C onclusion: Nurturing Kidney Health Through Knowledge and Support
As we draw the curtain on this exploration of Chronic Kidney Disease (CKD) and its various dimensions, it becomes clear that empowering individuals with knowledge and fostering a supportive environment are paramount in the journey toward kidney health. Throughout this comprehensive guide, we've delved into the intricacies of CKD, covering aspects ranging from dietary considerations and exercise practices to emotional well-being and community support.

A Holistic Approach to Kidney Health

The foundation of this guide rests on the principle that kidney health is not solely a medical matter; it is a holistic pursuit that encompasses physical, mental, and emotional well-being. The intricacies of navigating CKD require more than clinical intervention; they demand a comprehensive approach that empowers individuals to actively participate in their health journey.

Key Takeaways

1. Dietary Considerations

Understanding the nuances of nutrition is crucial in managing CKD effectively. From low-sodium and low-phosphorus cooking tips to selecting the right beverages and adjusting one's diet according to CKD changes, informed dietary choices play a pivotal role.

2. Physical Activity and Exercise Practices

Striking a balance between maintaining physical activity and adhering to safe exercise practices is essential for individuals with CKD. The benefits of regular physical activity on kidney health are profound and underscore the importance of an active lifestyle.

3. Emotional Well-being

The emotional impact of CKD should not be underestimated. Recognizing the emotional connection to nutrition and addressing psychosocial aspects are integral components of comprehensive CKD management. Support organizations, such as the National Kidney Foundation and The Renal Support Network, play a vital role in nurturing emotional well-being.

4. Community and Connection

Building a sense of community and connection is indispensable for individuals facing the challenges of CKD. Support organizations like Dialysis Patient Citizens and the Kidney Community Emergency Response Coalition contribute to this sense of belonging, offering opportunities for patients to share experiences and insights.

5. Information Dissemination

Access to accurate information is a cornerstone of effective CKD management. Support organizations, such as the American Association of Kidney Patients and the International Society of Nephrology, bridge knowledge gaps by providing educational resources and advocating for awareness.

Looking Ahead: Empowering Futures

In concluding this guide, we emphasize the power of knowledge, the importance of emotional well-being, and the strength derived from community support. Navigating the complexities of CKD is not a solitary endeavor; it is a collective effort that involves individuals, families, healthcare professionals, and support organizations working together.

By fostering an environment where accurate information is readily available, where emotional well-being is prioritized, and where individuals affected by CKD feel supported, we pave the way for empowered futures. Kidney health is not just a medical condition to be managed; it is a journey to be navigated with resilience, knowledge, and a supportive community by one's side.

As we move forward, let this guide serve as a resource and a source of inspiration for those on the path to kidney health. May it empower individuals to make informed choices, foster connections within communities, and contribute to a future where kidney health is synonymous with well-being and vitality.

| Page

www.ingramcontent.com/pod-product-compliance
Lightning Source LLC
Chambersburg PA
CBHW070923290526
45795CB00001B/398